W9-BZV-971

THE NATCHEZ TRACE HISTORIC TRAIL IN AMERICAN HISTORY

The In American History Series

IN
AMERICAN
HISTORY

THE NATCHEZ TRACE HISTORIC TRAIL IN AMERICAN HISTORY

William R. Sanford

Enslow Publishers, Inc.

40 Industrial Road   PO Box 38
Box 398   Aldershot
Berkeley Heights, NJ 07922   Hants GU12 6BP
USA   UK

http://www.enslow.com

Library of Congress Cataloging-in-Publication Data

Sanford, William R. (William Reynolds), 1927–
The Natchez Trace Historic Trail in American history / William R. Sanford.
     p. cm. — (In American history)
   Includes bibliographical references and index.
   Summary: Traces the history of this ancient trail used originally by
Native Americans, describes its use by travelers returning north from New
Orleans, and includes information about it as a national reserve.
   ISBN 0-7660-1344-8
   1. Natchez Trace—History—Juvenile literature. 2. Natchez Trace
National Scenic Trail—Juvenile literature. 3. Frontier and pioneer life—
Alabama—Juvenile literature. 4. Frontier and pioneer life—Tennessee—
Juvenile literature. 5. Frontier and pioneer life—Tennessee—Juvenile
literature. [1. Natchez Trace—History. 2. Natchez Trace National Scenic
Trail. 3. Frontier and pioneer life. 4. National parks and reserves.]
   I. Titles. II. Series.
F217.N37 S26   2001
976—dc21
                                   99-050646

Printed in the United States of America

10 9 8 7 6 5 4 3 2 1

To Our Readers: We have done our best to make sure all Internet addresses in
this book were active and appropriate when we went to press. However, the
author and the publisher have no control over and assume no liability for the
material available on those Internet sites or on other Web sites they may link to.
Any comments or suggestions can be sent by e-mail to comments@enslow.com or
to the address on the back cover.

Illustration Credits: Nashville, p. 63; Natchez CVB, pp. 51, 52, 54,
55; The Hermitage, p. 65, 66, 84; UNITED STATES PARK SERVICE,
pp. 9, 11, 13, 15, 16, 18, 21, 28, 40, 69, 72, 78, 89, 91, 93, 95, 99, 101,
102, 103; Western History Collections, University of Oklahoma
Libraries, p. 22; William R. Sanford, p. 6.

Cover Illustrations: The Hermitage; UNITED STATES PARK
SERVICE.

★ CONTENTS ★

*A trace is a kind of path or trail. The Natchez Trace—
extending from Natchez, Mississippi, to Nashville,
Tennessee—was heavily used for nearly fifty years before the
invention of the steamboat.*

In 1783, the United States and England signed a treaty ending the Revolutionary War. The treaty gave the United States a new western boundary north of present-day Louisiana: the Mississippi River. Colonists poured into the territory west of the Appalachian Mountains. Soon they were taking their surplus

TRAVELING THE NATCHEZ TRACE

goods down the Ohio and Mississippi rivers to Natchez, Mississippi, and New Orleans, Louisiana. To return home, it was necessary to travel on foot or on horseback. The Mississippi River flows downstream, and before the invention of the steamboat it was nearly impossible to row back upstream. Many walked along the Natchez Trace. For the traveler who walked about twenty miles a day, the return trip up the Natchez Trace could last over three weeks. A trace is a path or a trail. The Trace was an ancient trail used by American Indians. It stretched from Natchez, Mississippi, to Nashville, Tennessee, across what would become three states: Mississippi, Alabama, and Tennessee. Heavy use of the trail lasted for less than fifty years.

Preparing for the Trip

The starting point for most returning boatmen was Natchez-Under-The-Hill, Natchez's waterfront section. It catered to the tastes of river travelers. Natchez-Under-The-Hill lay below the bluffs lining the east bank of the Mississippi River. This section of town consisted largely of stores, saloons, and gambling establishments. Here travelers bought food for the journey north, stocking up on flour, bacon, dried beans, and rice. Many bought "travelers' bread;" biscuits resembling the hardtack common aboard sailing ships.

If travelers had a little extra money, they bought coffee and sugar. A pint per traveler of powdered Indian corn served as an emergency ration. A person could survive on a spoonful a day without feeling too hungry. Experienced hunters hoped to supplement their diets with turkey, deer, and other game. Those willing to risk being stung sought out beehives for honey.

Traveling in Groups

Most travelers tried to protect themselves from attacks by robbers. They formed themselves into groups of fifteen to twenty persons. On the trail, they traveled single file. This was a slow way to travel, because whatever may have delayed one traveler delayed all. Often those in a hurry took added risks, forging on in smaller groups.

The many springs and brooks that dotted the trail were favored campsites for weary travelers.

Travel was heaviest during the warmer months. Most of the horses on the Trace were small. They came from mixed Spanish and American Indian breeds. These Appaloosa horses could exist on grass and the bark of trees. On average, there was one horse to carry the baggage of every three or four people. Few of the horses made the trip without extreme fatigue. They usually reached their destination in poor condition. Many became ill from colic, a disease that attacks the colon, and died on the way.

Travelers rose at daybreak. Handcuff-like leather or iron hobbles had kept the horses nearby during the night. Though heavier to carry, iron hobbles were preferred because thieves could not easily cut them and steal the horses. Rounding up their horses, the travelers removed the hobbles from their horses' forefeet. Then they loaded the horses with their packs of goods and started up the Trace. By eleven o'clock A.M., men and animals were ready for rest. A fire would be lit, and loads were removed from the horses. The men and animals rested for a couple of hours. The process was repeated in the afternoon. By sundown, the travelers were ready to eat and turn in for the night.

Finding Food and Shelter

For many years, travelers on the Trace slept by the roadside. They found few places to rent a bed for the night. Later such sites became plentiful. Frontier businessmen built cabins called *stands*. There a traveler could buy a meal or spend the night. The first stands were located near Natchez, Mississippi. Six miles north of Natchez was the inn at Washington. Six miles farther north was Selsertown, where three of the ten houses in the village were taverns. Sixty miles from Natchez was Grindstone Ford, the last of the settlements before the wilderness. Travelers shared the one room cabins with their goods, the owner, and his few articles of rough furniture. Supper most often was boiled milk and corn mush. Some found the overcrowding unbearable, and chose to spread their blankets outdoors.[1]

In northeast Mississippi, the travelers bought food from the Chickasaw Indians. From time to time, they

During the height of the Trace's use, cabins called "stands" were built. These one room rest areas provided exhausted travelers with food and shelter for the night.

★ 11 ★

could buy dried beef and venison. The "Indian bread" they bought was a type of corn bread. The Chickasaw sold their surplus milk to the travelers. Their home-made cheese was made from milk cooked in an iron kettle. White travelers who tried it reported that a person would have to be very hungry to take a bite, chew, and swallow.

The Chickasaw were very hospitable to travelers. If visitors entered one of their homes, they were offered cooked food. The Chickasaw took offense if the offered food was refused.

Travelers fascinated the Chickasaw. They paid particular attention to their horses and baggage. When they visited the Chickasaw villages, travelers kept a careful eye on their packs. To the Chickasaw, stealing from the travelers was a game. When they succeeded, they could brag and joke about it. If they were caught, they were merely disappointed, not ashamed.

Sometimes storms blew down trees, hiding the Trace. The Chickasaw were willing to serve as guides when this happened. During the early years of the Trace, travelers stocked up at the Chickasaw villages. There was little chance of buying food for hundreds of miles, because the next stand was only a few miles south of Nashville.

Crossing Creeks and Rivers

Wherever possible, the Trace followed high ground. It ran along ridgelines and skirted bluffs. Looking down, travelers often saw groups of ancient mounds—large monuments made of earth. The Trace itself seemed to lead from one group of mounds to the next. The travelers on the Trace had to cross many brooks, creeks, and rivers. Sometimes there was a ferry, consisting of a rough raft attached to a rope stretching across the stream. For a fee, the operator allowed travelers to board. Then, the ferryman pushed out from the bank. The current carried the raft to the opposite shore.

There was not any ferry service across the Tennessee River before 1800. Travelers had to swim to lead the animals across. Water soaked the goods in their packs. There was also the danger that the swift current would carry the horses downstream. Instead,

Before 1800, ferry service across rivers, like the Tennessee River, did not exist. Settlers would either have to swim across or make rafts to carry their goods and horses.

travelers often chose to take the time to build a raft. The process took a day or more. The travelers had to cut down trees. Then, the trunks were cut into six- to eight-foot sections. Wild grapevines served as ropes to bind the logs together. Sheets of bark served to form a deck. When the rafts were complete, the packs were loaded on board.

Travelers used their horses to pull the raft upstream. They waded into the stream as far as possible. Then, with ropes attached to the raft, they began swimming across the stream. The current took them downstream. If they were successful, they reached the landing on the opposite bank.

In 1801, the Chickasaw signed a treaty with the United States. They gave the United States the right-of-way for the Natchez Trace. By treaty, only the Chickasaw had the right to operate inns and ferries in the territory. The treaty did not forbid the Chickasaw from going into business with white partners, though. In 1802, George Colbert set up a ferry and inn by the Trace, at the crossing of the Tennessee River. Colbert charged high prices, but the Chickasaw rode for free.

The Trace continued northeast for two hundred miles from the Tennessee River. The final portion of the trail was rough and hilly. It was not until the traveler was within six miles of Nashville that the wilderness opened. Joslin's Plantation offered a taste of civilization. Wayfarers could buy a meal of boiled bacon, cornbread, and French beans.

The Tennessee River was not the only water obstacle along the Natchez Trace. John Gordon chose to create a ferry across the Duck River. His home along the bank of the river still stands today.

The Government Improves the Natchez Trace

The U.S. government needed to keep in touch with its most distant provinces. Secretary of State Timothy Pickering reported that a letter from Natchez took three months to reach him. In January 1800, the Postmaster General set up a mail service on the Trace. For $2,400 a year, Abijah Hunt would provide one round trip per month. The first riders carried newspapers, government dispatches, and personal letters. They all fit in a deerskin pouch waterproofed with oil.

The riders carried their own food and a horn to announce their arrival. They also carried half a bushel of corn for their horses.

The riders departed every other Sunday from Nashville. Their schedule called for them to cover 230 miles in six days. At Hookly Creek, the Nashville riders would meet riders coming up from Natchez. They would rest for a day, exchange mail, and return. A letter traveled from one end of the Trace to the other in two weeks.[2]

In 1802, the government began widening portions of the Natchez Trace. They widened the northern

In 1802, the United States government began improvements along the Trace. The workers widened, cleared, and leveled the path as much as possible, in order to make the journey more comfortable for travelers.

stretch first. Workers cleared a section between the Tennessee River and the Duck River. Then the crews extended their work north to Nashville. James Wilkinson was the military commander on the western frontier. In 1803, he sent some of his troops to Natchez. From there the soldiers began working their way north. They cleared a path eight feet wide. All trees were cut to leave stumps close to the ground. They made the surface as level as possible. The soldiers cleared the brush from another four feet on each side. Wilkinson replaced the work crews with new ones every thirty days. The soldiers' work provided travelers on foot and horseback with an easier trip on a well-marked road, but the Trace was not yet suitable for wheeled vehicles.

The work took longer than expected. After three years' work, the road from Natchez was finished for about forty miles to Grindstone Ford. For the next forty miles, the soldiers had cleared the right-of-way, but not the brush. That left a 186-mile gap to the Tennessee River. Postmaster General Gideon Granger divided the unfinished right-of-way into three sections. He contracted with civilian firms to clear a twelve-foot swath. All stumps were cut to eighteen inches or less above the ground. Bridges crossed streams less than forty feet wide. Larger rivers had graded banks, that made passage easier. Causeways were designed to cross swamps. By 1809, the work was done, and the Natchez Trace had become a wagon road.

By 1809 the Natchez trace was clear enough to become a wagon trail. Today, portions of the Trace still remain, although some sections have been paved for cyclists and joggers.

★ THE LINCOLNS, FATHER AND SON, GO TO NEW ORLEANS ★

Thomas Lincoln was twenty-eight years old in 1806. Born in Virginia, he lived in Hardin County, Kentucky. He owned his two-hundred-acre farm free of debt. In March, the firm of Bleakley & Montgomery hired Lincoln. The merchants wanted him to build a flatboat. When he finished it, they hired Lincoln to take a load of merchandise to New Orleans. Lincoln agreed. He and Isaac Bush headed the flatboat down the Ohio and Mississippi rivers. Their trip was a success. They sold the goods in New Orleans, and the flatboat was chopped up as usual and sold for lumber, because there was no easy way for travelers to get the flatboats back upstream.

Then Lincoln and Bush began the long walk back. They followed well-worn trails from New Orleans to Natchez. They then followed the Natchez Trace to Nashville. Other trails led them across Tennessee and Kentucky. Amazingly, they completed the round trip in two months. Lincoln used some of the money he had earned to pay for a wedding suit. He married twenty-two-year-old Nancy Hanks in June. The couple's first child, Sarah, was born in 1807. Their first son, Abraham, followed two years later.

When he was nineteen, Abraham Lincoln lived in Indiana. His mother and sister had died recently, and he seized a chance to get away. Storekeeper James Gentry wanted to send a flatboat to New Orleans. Gentry's son Allen would be in charge. Lincoln would earn $8 a month as a crewman. Abraham asked Thomas Lincoln many questions: What were the problems and pitfalls he would face? What was New Orleans like?[3]

In October 1828, Lincoln and Gentry began building the flatboat. Early in 1829, they set out with pork, flour, bacon, meal, potatoes, and produce. By day, Lincoln was at the bow, the front of the boat. He operated the oaks used for steering. They tied up to a riverbank tree each night, to keep the boat from floating away. Below Baton Rouge, Louisiana, they were near the Duquesne plantation. A gang of seven robbers boarded the flatboat to steal the cargo. Lincoln and Gentry fought them off. Lincoln received a gash over one eye, a scar he carried for life.

In New Orleans, the young men sold their cargo and the flatboat. They used the money to buy tobacco, cotton, and pants. Unlike his father, Lincoln did not have to walk home via the Natchez Trace. After a few days in New Orleans, Lincoln and Gentry took passage on a northbound steamboat. They had crossed half the United States. For Lincoln, it seemed like it was a three-month paid vacation.[4]

★ THE MOUNDBUILDERS LEAVE A MYSTERY BEHIND THEM ★

When European settlers entered the Mississippi basin, they found hundreds of giant earthen mounds. Clearly, they were man-made in an earlier time. Some were huge. The Cahokia Mound in Illinois was one hundred feet tall and covered sixteen acres. Others were low and elaborate. Their builders made them in the shape of animals. Inside some were human bones, weapons, tools, and jewelry. The area of the Natchez Trace was rich with these abandoned structures. Who made them? What was their use?

The Europeans jumped to a wrong conclusion. The Indians in the region were few in numbers. They showed no signs of ever having moved and shaped tons of earth. The Europeans surmised that the mounds had been built by a vanished race. Some suggested the lost tribes of Israel. After all, the Old Testament described the worship of the Canaanites and Israelites in "high places." Other candidates were the Vikings, Greeks, Persians, Romans, Hindus, and Phoenicians.[5]

Modern archeology tells a different story. A series of Mound Builder cultures created the monuments. The earliest, now called the Adena, built cone-shaped burial mounds. The Adena lived in the Ohio Valley about 1000 B.C. A new group, the Hopewell, arrived from the eastern

Travelers of the Natchez Trace were often mystified by giant mounds built along the trail. American Indians constructed these giant mounds for ceremonial purposes. Emerald Mound is the second largest such mound in the country.

woodlands about 400 B.C. The Hopewell built larger mounds in which they buried their dead. Some graves contained jewelry of bone, shell, and stone. In others were copper breastplates, headdresses, and mica ornaments. The Hopewell sites showed many Mexican influences. It is likely that ideas flowed from Mexico to the Mississippi River basin. By A.D. 550, the Hopewell ceased building their sites. By A.D. 750, the area was depopulated. No one knows why. Possible causes include climate change, civil war, and outside invasion.

Around A.D. 900, mound building began again in the Southeast. These mounds were different from the

IN THE EARLY 1800S, THE SHAWNEE CHIEF TECUMSEH INVITED THE CHOCTAW TO JOIN IN A GRAND ALLIANCE AGAINST THE AMERICANS. CHOCTAW CHIEF PUSHMATAHA REPLIED:

THESE WHITE AMERICANS BUY OUR SKINS, OUR CORN, OUR COTTON, OUR SURPLUS GAME, OUR BASKETS AND OTHER WARES. . . . THEY GIVE US [IN] FAIR EXCHANGE THEIR CLOTH, THEIR GUNS, THEIR TOOLS, IMPLEMENTS, AND OTHER THINGS WHICH THE CHOCTAW NEED BUT DO NOT MAKE. IT IS TRUE WE HAVE BEFRIENDED THEM, BUT WHO WILL DENY THAT THESE ACTS OF FRIENDSHIP HAVE BEEN ABUNDANTLY RECIPROCATED? THEY HAVE GIVEN US COTTON GINS, WHICH SIMPLIFY THE SPINNING AND SALE OF OUR COTTON. THEY HAVE ENCOURAGED AND HELPED US IN THE PRODUCTION OF OUR CROPS. THEY HAVE TAKEN MANY OF OUR WIVES INTO THEIR HOMES TO TEACH THEM USEFUL THINGS. [THEY] PAY THEM FOR THEIR WORK WHILE LEARNING. YOU ALL REMEMBER WELL THE DREADFUL EPIDEMIC VISITED UPON US LAST WINTER. DURING ITS DARKEST HOURS THESE NEIGHBORS WHOM WE ARE NOW URGED TO ATTACK RESPONDED GENEROUSLY TO OUR NEEDS. THEY DOCTORED OUR SICK. THEY CLOTHED OUR SUFFERING. THEY FED OUR HUNGRY. . . . IT WILL BE SEEN THAT THE WHITES AND INDIANS IN THIS SECTION ARE LIVING ON FRIENDLY AND MUTUALLY BENEFICIAL TERMS."[6]

Choctaw chief Pushmataha rejected Shawnee Chief Tecumseh's offer of alliance against white settlers. Pushmataha believed that American Indians and whites could live together and help one another.

Hopewell structures. They were used as platforms for temples, not burials. The earthen mounds rose eighty to one hundred feet. Atop them, the builders erected wooden structures.

The Temple Mound Builders were excellent farmers. They tilled the earth with hoes made from shell, stone, or the shoulder blades of animals. Their culture spread from Illinois to the Gulf Coast. Yet, by the end of the 1600s, all of the major Temple Mound Builder sites were abandoned.

It is likely that the Creek, Chickasaw, and Choctaw were the descendants of the Temple Mound Builders. By the time white people arrived, this part of their culture was long forgotten.

2

AMERICAN INDIANS OF THE NATCHEZ TRACE

The first migrants are thought to have arrived in North America roughly fifteen thousand years ago. They crossed an ice bridge from Siberia to Alaska. It took three or four thousand years for them to reach the Mississippi Valley. Coming to the area via the eastern woodlands, their descendants already knew how to plant corn, beans, squash, and melons. They domesticated chickens and hunted bison. They lived in the Mississippi Valley's western forests, where wood was plentiful for building homes and making fires. Today, historians know these people as the Muskogee.

In time, the Muskogee split into smaller groups. The two largest were the Chicasha (Chickasaw) and the Chacta (Choctaw). The largest, the Choctaw, had twenty thousand people, scattered among seventy or so villages. They were fierce and well organized. They absorbed smaller groups into their "nations." Many small groups occupied the eastern bank of the Mississippi River. On the bluffs above the river were a half dozen villages, where an estimated twelve hundred people lived. The names of the groups living there were the Alabama, the Houma, the Mobilieu, the Tunica, and the Colapissa.[1]

The Natchez

A different tribe, the Natchez, lived in the southwest of what is now the state of Mississippi. The first recorded contact between the Natchez and Europeans took place in 1542. The Spanish explorer Hernando De Soto reported that a mound-building, sun-worshiping people dominated the Natchez area. French explorer Sieur de La Salle reported their presence over a century later. White Apple Village, ten miles south of present Natchez, was the center of tribal activity. Of all the tribes in North America, the Natchez were unique. They were the only ones with an absolute monarch. The Great Sun and his relatives, also called Suns, formed the nobility. At the other end of the social scale were the common people, unhappily known in English as *stinkards*.[2]

The tribe numbered about four thousand to 4,500 in 1650. The Natchez had the most advanced culture of the southeastern tribes. They were skilled farmers and craftsmen. Probably descendants of the earlier Temple Mound Builders, the Natchez maintained the rites and ceremonies at the temple mounds into historic time.[3]

The French set up a trading post, Fort Rosalie, in Natchez territory in 1713. In 1729, the Natchez felt that the French commandant had insulted their chief.

The Natchez attacked the post, killing about two hundred of its inhabitants. The French were quick to take revenge. With their Choctaw allies, they attacked the Natchez. Four hundred Natchez surrendered. The French sold them into slavery in the West Indies. The other Natchez fled to live with the Creek, Chickasaw, and Cherokee. Today, all that remains of the tribe is the name.

The Choctaw

The Choctaw lived in Alabama and Mississippi. They were an agricultural people who raised corn, beans, sunflowers, melons, and squash. From the Europeans, the Choctaw learned to raise cotton. They spun and wove the cotton for their clothes. Many of the Choctaw raised fowl and livestock. In their fields, they produced fruit and vegetables. The Choctaw exported their surplus to other tribes. They were peaceable, fighting only to defend themselves. Their houses arched over pole frames. Over the frames, the Choctaw fastened woven mats. Often, clay and crushed shells formed an outer coat. Many families had two homes, one for winter and one for summer. The summer homes were open on all sides. Winter homes had an interior firepit. Water poured on hot stones provided a kind of steam heat.

Religion, while important, was not central to the Choctaw. They worshiped a supreme being, Hush-tali, a god related to the sun. Their religion included elaborate death rituals. The tribe divided itself into geographic regions. Each region had its own chief and council. Within a region, farming families organized towns. The Choctaw organized their people into two social groups, the *Inhulata* and the *Kashapa Okla*. The division crossed regional boundaries. Within each social group were several clans. Marriages took place outside the clan. Children belonged to their mother's clan, and raising them was the mother's clan's responsibility. Fathers had no control over the children.[4] Women made clothing, prepared food, and tended the fields. Men manufactured stone tools and built the homes. They hunted, and provided for the tribe's defense.

The Choctaw were important allies of the French. They opposed the British colonists during the French and Indian War. After the United States became independent, the Choctaw proved themselves good friends. A Shawnee chief asked the Choctaw to join him in attacking the white settlers. The Choctaw refused. They fought on the American side in the War of 1812. Choctaw warriors fought on the side of Andrew Jackson in the Battle of New Orleans in 1815. The Choctaw were prosperous, they occupied rich farmlands, and many had intermarried with whites. Still, none of this saved the Choctaw. They became the first victims of the Indian Removal Law.

Through bribes and coercion, the Choctaw agreed to the Treaty of Dancing Rabbit Creek. By the terms of this 1830 treaty, they gave up 10.5 million acres in Mississippi. The U.S. government required them to

The native Choctaw once raised corn, beans, sunflowers, melons, and squash in many of the fields along the Natchez Trace. Today, farmers still tend crops in these same fields.

move to Oklahoma. Thirteen thousand Choctaw began the 550-mile trek. Four thousand of them died of hunger, exposure, and disease. Seven thousand refused to move. They remained in Mississippi, subject to state laws. The state promptly passed a new law saying the tribe no longer existed.

The Chickasaw

The Chickasaw were a small tribe of fewer than four thousand members, with each of their eight bands ruled by a male chief. Their eight villages were in Mississippi, Alabama, and Tennessee. The villages stood on high ground near stands of hardwood trees. Their homes were framed with poles. Over them were coverings of grass thatch, cane, bark, or hide. Each household had a winter and a summer house. The Chickasaw engaged in limited farming. They raised corn, melon, and pumpkins. They also were skilled traders with other tribes. At one time, the Chickasaw language was widespread. The lower Mississippi tribes used it for commerce and contact between tribes.

The Chickasaw were closely related to the Choctaw. The two tribes spoke dialects of the Muscogean language. The Chickasaw were an energetic and warlike people. Their first contact with Europeans was between 1540 and 1541. Spanish explorer Hernando De Soto demanded that the Chickasaw provide him with two hundred women to use as carriers. Instead, the Chickasaw attacked de Soto. The Spaniards lost eleven men, fifty-seven horses, and four hundred pigs.[5] The Chickasaw remained largely undisturbed for the next 150 years.

Around 1700, the Chickasaw found themselves between two groups of Europeans. English traders crossed the Appalachians and reached Chickasaw lands. French settlements began near the mouth of the Mississippi. The Chickasaw allied themselves with the English. The tribe fought against the French and their Choctaw allies. During the Revolutionary War, the Chickasaw fought with the colonists against the British. From this time on, many Chickasaw women married white traders and settlers.

The Chickasaw were intensely religious. They followed a lunar calendar in which each full moon was a time for celebration. Their social organization resembled that of the Choctaw. One difference was that, while the women raised the girls, the men raised the boys.

In 1786, the Treaty of Hopewell, a treaty between the United States and the Chickasaw, established the borders of Chickasaw territory. Between 1805 and 1818, the Chickasaw ceded their land in western Tennessee to the United States. By 1822, the Chickasaw began to migrate west. By 1837, most tribal members lived in the Indian Territory (present-day Oklahoma).

Other Tribes in the Region

The Creek occupied the northeastern part of the region, with some of their villages in southern Tennessee. Warfare was a part of their way of life. The Creek allied themselves with the British during the Revolution. They attacked frontier settlements in Tennessee as early as 1780. In 1795, the Chickasaw defeated the Creek near the Tombigbee River. Andrew Jackson commented, "When the whole Creek nation came to destroy your town, . . . a few hundred Chickasaw . . . chased them back to their nation, killing the best of their warriors, and covering the rest with shame."[6]

The Shawnee were relative newcomers to the region. They lived in southern Ohio, Pennsylvania, and

THE BOUNDARY OF LANDS HEREBY ALLOTTED TO THE CHICKASAW NATION TO LIVE AND HUNT ON . . . BEGINNING ON THE RIDGE THAT DIVIDES THE WATERS RUNNING INTO THE CUMBERLAND, FROM THOSE RUNNING INTO THE TENNESSEE, AT A POINT IN A LINE TO BE RUN NORTH-EAST, WHICH SHALL STRIKE THE TENNESSEE AT THE MOUTH OF DUCK RIVER; THENCE RUNNING WESTERLY ALONG SAID RIDGE, TILL IT SHALL STRIKE THE OHIO; THENCE DOWN THE SOUTHERN BANKS THEREOF TO THE MISSISSIPPI; THENCE DOWN THE SAME, TO THE CHOCTAW LINE OR THE NATCHEZ DISTRICT; THENCE ALONG THE SAID LINE, OR THE LINE OF THE DISTRICT EASTWARD AS FAR AS THE CHICKASAWS CLAIMED, AND LIVED AND HUNTED ON, THE TWENTY-NINTH OF NOVEMBER, ONE THOUSAND SEVEN HUNDRED AND EIGHTY-TWO. THENCE THE SAID BOUNDARY, EASTWARDLY SHALL BE THE LANDS ALLOTTED TO THE CHOCTAWS AND CHEROKEES TO LIVE AND HUNT ON, AND THE LANDS AT PRESENT IN THE POSSESSION OF THE CREEKS; SAVING AND RESERVING FOR THE ESTABLISHMENT OF A TRADING POST. . .AT THE LOWER PORT OF THE MUSCLE SHOALS. . .TO BE USED AND UNDER THE GOVERNMENT OF THE UNITED STATES OF AMERICA.[7]

The young United States established the Chickasaw boundaries in the Treaty of Hopewell on January 10, 1786.

West Virginia until about 1660. Then they were driven out by the Iroquois. Some moved for a short time to the Cumberland River basin of Tennessee. Most had returned to the northeast by 1730.

The Cherokee claimed the area at the northern end of the Natchez Trace, but they did not live there. De Soto reported contact with the Cherokee on the Tennessee River. Most of the tribe's two hundred villages were farther to the east. The Cherokee heartland included the southern Appalachian Mountains in North and South Carolina. Other groups lived in Virginia, Georgia, Alabama, Kentucky, and Tennessee.

In 1760, the thirteen British colonies stretched along the coast of the Atlantic Ocean. The Appalachian Mountains, formed the western boundary of the colonies. Settlement stretched inland only a hundred miles or less. Hostile French colonies in Canada lay to the north. To the south, Spanish Florida blocked expansion.

THE UNITED STATES 1760–1800

In a way, this suited the colonies' British rulers just fine. Their colonies showed signs of resisting British laws and taxes. It would be easier to control them if they were within easy range of the coast and the British Navy. In 1763, the British issued a new law. The Proclamation Act limited the colonies to lands east of the Appalachians.[1]

The Revolution Brings New Boundaries

Twenty years later, much had changed. England had won the French and Indian War (1756–63). The Canadian colonies became British. French agents vanished from the frontier. No longer could they encourage American Indians to raid British settlements. In 1776, the Thirteen Colonies pro-claimed independence. The Revolutionary War (1776–83) ended in American victory. The Proclamation of 1763 was law no longer. The colonists were free to expand to the west.

The Treaty of Paris ended the Revolutionary War. Britain gave up its land claims west of the Appalachians. The western boundary of the United States became the Mississippi River.[2] Before the Revolution, several colonies claimed western lands. North of the Ohio River, Connecticut, Massachusetts, New York, and Virginia had land claims. South of the Ohio River, Virginia, North Carolina, South Carolina, and Georgia claimed western lands. One by one, the new states surrendered their claims to the United States. Between 1781 and 1802, the states ceded over 236 million acres to the federal government.[3] The lands west of the Appalachians were open for colonization.

The nation passed two laws dealing with the new lands. The Land Ordinance of 1785 provided for surveying the land. It provided for townships, each six miles square, and placed land for sale in 640-acre plots at $1 per acre.[4] The Northwest Ordinance (1787) provided for admission of new states from western lands. Each would rank as an equal with the original thirteen.[5] Kentucky would become the first new state created from the western lands joining the Union in 1792.

The Country Organizes a New Government

During the Revolution, the United States had two weak national governments. For most of the war (1775–81), the Second Continental Congress ruled the land. There was no chief executive to lead the country. There was no national court system. The thirteen states were jealous of each other. They had trouble reaching agreement. The Congress had trouble collecting taxes. It ordered the printing of millions in paper money, but the bills soon became almost worthless.

In 1777, Congress approved the Articles of Confederation. It took four years for all thirteen states to ratify them. There would be a new national legislature. Each state, large or small, would have one vote. The government lacked the power to tax the people. It could not regulate interstate commerce. It lacked a strong military, and the country still lacked a chief executive and federal judges. The country needed a stronger national government.

In 1787, a convention met in Philadelphia. There, the Constitution was written and submitted to the state governments. A president, elected for four years, would be the chief executive. He would head the administrative agencies. These included the State Department, Treasury Department, War Department, and Post Office Department. The new Congress would have two branches. Each state would have two members in the Senate. A state's population determined its share of members in the House of Representatives. A Supreme Court would head a federal judicial system. The required nine states ratified the Constitution in 1788. The young nation elected George Washington as its first president. He served two terms (1789–97). His vice president, John Adams, followed him as president (1797–1801).

Treaties Support Westward Growth

Two treaties brought peace with the new nation's northern and western neighbors. Jay's Treaty (1794) eased tensions between the United States and Britain. Ten years after the Revolution, the British still occupied six frontier forts in American territory. The forts lay along the river and lake boundary with Canada. They slowed the settlement of the west. They also kept control of the fur trade in British hands. Americans in the Ohio country believed American Indian attacks were supported by the British. By the terms of Jay's Treaty, the British agreed to evacuate the forts within two years.

The treaty's provisions were also secured by a military victory. In August, General Anthony Wayne led an army of two thousand regular soldiers and a thousand Kentucky volunteers into the Ohio country. Two thousand Wyandot warriors opposed them. They occupied a two-mile line in a forest blown down by a hurricane. The Battle of Fallen Timbers ended in American victory. The Wyandot scattered, some retreating to a nearby British-held fort.

Pinckney's Treaty (1795) ended twelve years of dispute with Spain. Also called the Treaty of San Lorenzo, the agreement dealt with the United States' southern and western boundaries. In the treaty, Spain recognized the U.S. boundary claims. They were the Mississippi River to the west and the thirty-first parallel to the south. The treaty guaranteed the United States free navigation of the Mississippi River. It also gave Americans the right of deposit at the Spanish port of New Orleans. This meant Americans could ship their goods from New Orleans without paying Spanish taxes. Many of the Americans who floated their cargoes down the great river would walk home over the Natchez Trace.

The United States Grows in Population and New States

In 1790, the United States took its first census, which estimated the country's population at almost four million. About a million people lived in New England. The Middle Atlantic states were home to another million. Just under two million lived in the South Atlantic states. The country covered almost nine hundred thousand square miles, and was almost totally rural. Only two cities boasted over twenty-five thousand people. Only ten others had a population of over five thousand.[6]

Before the Revolution, both New York and New Hampshire claimed ownership of Vermont. In 1791, both states waived their claims. Vermont joined the union as the fourteenth state. In 1777, what is now known as Tennessee became Washington County,

North Carolina. The state of North Carolina ceded its western lands to the United States in 1784. Settlers in eastern Tennessee tried to declare their lands to be the state of Franklin. The effort failed. In 1790, the United States organized the area as the Territory South of the Ohio River. Tennessee joined the union as the fifteenth state on June 1, 1796.

The Nation Proves Democracy Works

The system of government contained in the U.S. Constitution was unique in the world. It called for separation of powers between the legislative, executive, and judicial branches. Congress added ten amendments to the Constitution, known as the Bill of Rights. The states had ratified all of the Bill of Rights by 1791. That year, Congress set up a Bank of the United States. It would issue money and collect taxes.

President Washington ran for a second term in 1792. His Federalist Party believed in a strong central government. The voters re-elected Washington. Washington's vice president, John Adams, won the presidency in the 1796 election. In 1798, the Congress passed the unpopular Alien and Sedition Laws. The laws aimed at limiting political opposition to the Federalists. The voters were unhappy. In 1800, they elected the Democratic Republican Thomas Jefferson as president. Adams and the Federalists yielded power peacefully. The American system of government worked.

From the nation's beginning, the issue of slavery divided the states. Before the Revolution, many states had begun freeing slaves. Four New England states emancipated their slaves by 1783. The Northwest Ordinance forbade slavery north of the Ohio River. At the Constitutional Convention of 1787, the delegates reached a compromise. Three-fifths of a state's slaves could be counted in determining congressional representation. The invention of the cotton gin by Eli Whitney in 1793 made slavery much more profitable. Cotton farming spread to the south and west. The economic well-being of the South became ever more firmly linked to slavery.

New Transportation Systems Develop

Before the Revolution, the country had a limited transportation system. Most commerce moved on water from seaport to seaport. Overland travel was slow and arduous. In 1794, Congress passed an act establishing post roads for the deliver of mail and stage transportation. The total mileage of post roads jumped from 5,001 when the law passed to 104,521 in 1829.[7] For the first time, mail service expanded into Tennessee and Kentucky.

Private companies began building toll roads. The Philadelphia-Lancaster Turnpike was completed in 1794. The following year, the Knoxville Road and the Wilderness Road were open to wagon traffic. That year the Old Walton Road extended from Knoxville to Nashville.

The canal building era began as well. In Massachusetts, a canal linked Boston with the Merrimac River. In 1796, a canal bypassed the falls of the Mohawk River in New York.

Land Speculators Play a Role in Settling the West

The words "western movement" commonly bring a number of images to mind: A family of pioneers would load their goods into a covered wagon, and work their way west. The father rode on horseback, his rifle at the ready. The wife drove the laboring team,

During the 1700s much of the land in the West was dense forest. Settlers had to clear the land in order to create homesteads. Clearing a field of trees was slow and very hard work.

while the children led a cow and a pig or two. The family would eventually go into the wilderness to create a homestead. First they built a rude cabin, and then they created their fields, cutting down one tree at a time.

There is one question not often asked about these pictures: Who owned the land on which they hoped to settle? The answer often was land speculators; people or companies who owned large amounts of land which they would sell for profit. They included the colonial leaders, Benjamin Franklin, Richard Henry Lee, and Robert and Gouverneur Morris. George Washington owned large amounts of land in Virginia, Ohio, and Pennsylvania. The lands controlled by speculators were sizeable. Georgia granted thirty million acres of land to four companies for one and a half cents per acre.[8]

Richard Henderson was a native of Virginia. In 1775, he was a retired judge living in North Carolina. He bought land between the Kentucky and Cumberland rivers from the Cherokee. He organized the Transylvania Land Company for the purpose of colonizing the area, hiring Daniel Boone to build a road to his new lands. Virginia and North Carolina both had claims to the land. The outbreak of the Revolution caused Henderson to abandon his plans. Four years later, he would try again. He financed the parties that settled at French Lick. The settlement became Nashville, northern terminus (endpoint) of the Natchez Trace.

★ DANIEL BOONE LEADS THE WAY WEST ★

In 1769, Daniel Boone was thirty-five. He lived on a farm in North Carolina. Years earlier, his friend John Finley had told him tales of a far-off paradise called Kentucky. Finley visited Boone's farm, and Boone agreed to lead Finley and four others on a westward trek. Boone passed through the Cumberland Gap, following an Indian trail that whites called the Warrior's Trace. A few weeks later, he stood on a hilltop north of the Kentucky River. He fell in love with the "wonderful land of Kentucke."[9] He remained there for six months, hunting deer and beaver. Then a Shawnee war party captured Boone. They did not harm him, but they took his hides and horses. His second trip in 1771 also ended in disaster. This time the Cherokee stole his horses and furs.

First Settlement in Kentucky

In March 1775, Boone agreed to build a road into Kentucky. Land speculator Richard Henderson promised to pay him two thousand acres of land. Boone gathered family and friends to do the work. The pay for the work crew was good—ten British pounds. Boone and his group marked the way along the Warrior's Trace. The crew felled trees, moved rocks, and cut brush. After two weeks work, they reached the Kentucky border. There, as Boone described it, "A party of Indians fired on my party about half an hour before day. [They] killed Mr. Twetty and his [servant]."[10] A second attack two days later took two more lives. On April 6, the road builders reached the Kentucky River. On the south bank, they built a cluster of log huts. To protect them, they raised a twelve-foot stockade. They called their settlement Fort Boone.

Boone and His Family Move West

Daniel Boone decided to bring his family to Kentucky. His wife, Rebecca, and their seven children arrived in September 1776. America had declared independence three months earlier. For seven years, the settlers fought the British and their Shawnee allies. After the war, Boone continued to move west. He worked for six years as a surveyor in Limestone, Kentucky. He later moved to Point Pleasant and then Brushy Fork. Finally, in 1799, Boone led his family across the Mississippi River, and settled in what is now Missouri, but at the time was Spanish territory. In Missouri, Boone served as a syndic—a sheriff, judge, and jury, all in one.

Daniel Boone lived to be eighty-five. He saw settlement spread south into Tennessee, and travel develop along the Natchez Trace.

4

SOUTHERN STARTING POINT OF THE TRACE

For those who traveled north up the Trace, their travels began at Natchez. The recorded history of the town stretches back over three hundred years.

Near the end of March 1683, the explorer René Robert Cavelier (known as Sieur de La Salle) and twenty-two other Frenchmen landed near Natchez. They smoked the pipe of peace with the Natchez chiefs before leaving the area. Forty years passed before the French returned. Then, in 1716, the French founded their first settlement in the Mississippi Valley. Jean Baptiste Le Moyne, known as Sieur de Bienville, established Fort Rosalie on high bluffs beside the river at Natchez.[1] The outpost was over 350 miles north of the mouth of the Mississippi River. Two years later, Bienville founded New Orleans on marshy ground three hundred miles to the south. For now, Bienville's mission was to conquer the Natchez. He had only forty-nine men to accomplish the job, but Bienville was ruthless. He captured the Great Sun, leader of the tribe. He forced the chief to surrender the leaders of a raid against the fort. These raiders were executed.

Natchez Suffers and Changes Hands

Bienville had chosen his site wisely. The land around Natchez was fertile. The climate made agriculture easy. The fevers common downstream were rare here. By 1720, the Natchez colony was home to three hundred colonists.

In 1729, the commander of Fort Rosalie was Sieur de Chopart. He was a greedy tyrant. He claimed more land from the Natchez people. His demand even included White Apple Village. The village contained ancient mounds where the Natchez performed ceremonies. On November 29, 1729, the Natchez came to the fort. They told the French that the Natchez's ancient enemies, the Choctaw, were about to attack. The French loaded guns and gave them to the Natchez. The Natchez had tricked the French. They used the weapons to attack the French settlers. One report listed 144 men, thirty-five women, and fifty-six children killed. The Natchez took a few women and slaves as prisoners.[2]

The French were quick to seek revenge. They enlisted the Choctaw as allies. From New Orleans, Governor Perier sent an avenging army. In February 1730, the French wiped out most of the Natchez tribe. Anyone captured by the French was sold into slavery in the West Indies. The area of the fort was almost deserted. Vines soon grew to cover the ruins of the settlers' cabins. In 1734, the French moved Fort Rosalie to a new location. It became a terraced fort atop the Natchez bluffs. Gradually, French families again began to settle at Natchez.

The French and Indian Wars ended in 1763. Britain was victorious, and in the peace treaty England received the east bank of the Mississippi. The French flag came down from Fort Rosalie. The British flag replaced it. The fort took on a new name, Fort Panmure. Natchez quickly became English in nature. Huge land grants went to retired soldiers. Some grants ranged from twenty-five hundred to five thousand acres.[3] In this "fourteenth English colony," gentry, or the upper-class males, wore powdered wigs. They slept under soft linen. Family portraits graced the walls of their homes. Bills of lading recorded imports of London porter (beer), white silk stockings, and pale blue stationery.

Natchez was part of a British province of West Florida. The British ruled it from Pensacola, Florida, and tried to encourage settlement in Natchez. They offered presents of large land grants to any who would settle there. Settlers came from as far away as New England. The English also imported African slaves to work the land.

Fighting in the Revolutionary War began at Lexington and Concord, Massachusetts, in 1775. The residents of Natchez did not join the colonies along the Atlantic. Loyalists from Georgia and the Carolinas moved into the area. In 1779, Spain allied itself with the Americans. The governor of Louisiana, Bernardo de Galvez, led a fleet of barges up the Mississippi. He captured the British fort at Baton Rouge, in what today is Louisiana. The British commander there agreed to the surrender of Natchez as well. Near the end of September, Galvez's forces reached Natchez. The British garrison surrendered as agreed. Soon the Spanish flag flew over Spanish Natchez.

The Spanish occupation of Natchez was brief. Spain sent very few Spaniards to the city. English remained the dominant language. Spain sent a few Irish priests to Natchez. The priests tried to convert Natchez residents to Catholicism, with little success.

The Revolutionary War ended in 1783. The peace treaty gave most of the east bank of the Mississippi to the United States. The area around Natchez became part of the United States after the signing of Pinckney's treaty in October 1795. The Americans did not take possession at once. It was February 1797 when the U.S. flag was first unfurled in sight of Fort Panmure.[4] The Spanish troops did not abandon the fort until March 1798, because the United States had sent only a few troops to Fort Panmure. Across the Mississippi River, Spain continued to rule for another five years.

The transfer to the United States did not much alter the form of government for Natchez. The president appointed the territorial governor, who ruled the territory along with a panel of three judges. The governor appointed the city's mayor, recorder, alderman, clerk, and marshal. They composed the Court of the City of Natchez. The Court enacted local laws. It collected fines of up to $50 for violations. The people elected six assistants, a treasurer, assessor, and a tax collector. The six assistants formed a Chamber of Representatives. They raised money by taxing property owners. The maximum tax was set at twenty-five cents per hundred dollars' assessed value.[5]

The first American governor was a Massachusetts sea captain, Winthrop Sargent. Arriving in Natchez ill, he disliked the city from the start. He found the climate and mosquitoes unbearable. Natchez's relaxed attitude offended his Puritan ideals. Sargent had no legal background, and no law books to guide him. The law in Natchez was confusing. What was the status now of Spanish and British land grants? To clarify the situation, Sargent issued a series of new laws. He forbade the sale of liquor to American Indians. He built a new jail. He created new taxes on tavern ownership, marriage licenses, and passports. Citizens urged his ouster, and when President Jefferson took office in 1801, Sargent went home to Massachusetts.

Natchez in the Early 1800s

By 1800, Natchez had become an important Mississippi River port. Its commerce ranked second behind New Orleans. Visitors thought it was one of the most handsome cities in the country. It was surrounded by forests where dozens of varieties of trees flourished.

The city of Natchez lay on high ground. The bluff was almost perpendicular to the shore. It rose about two hundred feet. At its foot was a narrow clay shelf between half to two-thirds of a mile long. Here, at Natchez-Under-The-Hill, was the Landing. A hundred or more riverboats could be tied at the wharf. A ferry crossed the Mississippi River. The wharf was most busy between October and early June. Summer brought low water that exposed snags and sandbars. Near the wharf was a straggling line of wooden buildings. Narrow streets crisscrossed randomly. Weather-beaten shacks crowded together. Others perched on stilts over the water's edge. Earlier, the Landing was more or less a quiet place. By 1800, it had become a place to gamble, drink, fight, and kill. One Natchez native moaned, "All of the bad reputation which Natchez acquired was after it came into the hands of the Americans."[6]

Natchez-Under-The-Hill was filled with drinking places. In these dives, dice rolled and music blared. Cardsharps hunched over tables. A boastful crewman might complain about a month passed without a fight. Outside, dim figures moved in the fog that rose from the river. Dark floating objects drifted downstream. No one checked to see whether there was any life left in them.

A steep path led up the cliff to Natchez itself. The crewmen who climbed it had money to spend. A keelboat captain earned a hundred dollars a month. His crewmen received half that. Natchez was ready to separate the boatmen from their money. In its early years, Natchez had a reputation for hospitality.

Residents had opened their homes to provide free lodging for travelers and boatmen. This was true no longer. Inns and taverns existed both below and atop the bluff. The food they offered reflected the times. Beef and pork tended to disappoint diners, but the Mississippi River catfish were superb. Some reached the amazing size of two hundred pounds.

In 1800, Natchez contained roughly three hundred houses. It boasted twenty-five hundred residents. Most of the houses were frame dwellings. The average home was about forty feet wide and eighteen feet deep. Houses faced the river to catch the westerly breezes. Many followed the dogtrot pattern—two large rooms flanked a large central hall. Larger homes were twenty by forty feet. They had paved galleries in front and behind. Arches and wrought iron grillwork reflected a Spanish influence. These homes contained a parlor, two bedrooms, two storage rooms, and a kitchen. Natchez homes came in a variety of colors. They included Spanish brown, chrome yellow, rose pink, Prussian blue, and verdigris green.

The main street ran east from the bluff. On the main street, merchants adorned their storefronts with goods to tempt the passerby. It seemed as if they turned their stores inside out every morning. Peddlers piled their merchandise at random, making pedestrians zigzag.

Most traffic on the street depended on horses. Men wearing wide-brimmed white hats and white blanket coats rode fine saddle horses. Ladies rode in carriages.

Plantation owners came to Natchez to buy and sell their products. For sport, they gambled on their horses at the local racetrack. They lounged about bars, or dined with cronies at inns. Slave sales always drew a big crowd. Many of the men tended to marry late, keeping their bachelor habits all their lives. Mixed in with the local citizenry were the Kentucky boatmen. Their rough linsey-woolsey clothing and long locks of hair made them easy to spot.

The city's economy was booming at this time. For miles around land had been cleared. Cotton, first grown from seed imported from Mexico, thrived. In

During the nineteenth century Natchez became one of the richest cities in America. Carriages carried ladies around town. Today, horse drawn carriages can still be seen in the historic district of Natchez.

1793, Connecticut inventor Eli Whitney created the cotton gin. The machine cleaned as much cotton as fifty people working by hand. Two years later, an African-American farmer named Barkley built the first cotton gin in Mississippi.[7]

Settlers streamed down the Natchez Trace. According to an 1817 census, twenty-three thousand black slaves and twenty-five thousand whites lived in the state, along with thirty-five thousand American Indians. In December of that year, Mississippi became the nation's twentieth state. Natchez proudly became the new state's capital. Plantations produced yields of

The mansion Auburn typifies the homes built by wealthy traders and planters in Natchez during the 1800s.

$5,000 to $20,000 a year.[8] Plantation owners used their income to buy the finest European imports. Within fifty years, Natchez would have more millionaires than any other American city.[9]

★ NATCHEZ DISPLAYS ITS HISTORIC HERITAGE ★

Natchez delights in showing visitors its heritage. Since 1932, visitors have flocked to the city for its twice-yearly Pilgrimages. The Spring Pilgrimages are in late March and April. Many come on the Pilgrimage to enjoy the city's historic home tours. Thirty-one antebellum (pre–Civil War) mansions open their doors to visitors. Many are private residences, closed to visitors at other times. Costumed hostesses welcome visitors to four homes each morning and four homes each afternoon throughout the Pilgrimage. Each half day's selection requires a separate tour pass.

During the spring Pilgrimages, visitors can spend their evenings enjoying one of three historical programs. On Wednesday, Friday, and Saturday evenings Natchez offers the annual Confederate Pageant. Two hundred local performers reenact scenes of the Old South. The pageant attempts to transport the audience to a romanticized long ago era. *Southern Exposure* is an entertaining stage comedy that pokes good-natured fun at Natchez and the Pilgrimage. The comedy plays daily except Monday and Wednesday. The Holy Family Choir presents "Southern Road to Freedom" Tuesdays, Thursdays, and Saturdays. It traces the African-American experience in Natchez from the colonial era to the present day.

Twice a year Natchez opens stately homes such as the Parsonage to visitors.

The Fall Pilgrimage is in October. Eighteen houses are open to the public. Visitors can see three homes in morning tours and four in the afternoon. The selection of homes changes daily. In the evenings, visitors can choose between a traditional "Mississippi Medicine Show" (Mondays, Wednesdays, Fridays, and Saturdays) or Amos Polk's Voices of Hope Spiritual Singers (Sundays, Tuesdays, Thursdays).

During December, Natchez offers "An Antebellum Holiday on the Mississippi." Thirteen homes are open to the public, each decorated for the holiday season. In the evening, "Longwood in Lights" allows visitors to drive through the grounds of the historic Longwood Plantation.

More than a dozen Natchez homes are open for touring year round. The choices vary by season. Tickets are available at Natchez Pilgrimage Tours, Canal Street Deport, at the corner of Canal and State Streets.

The United States Park Service maintains the Natchez National Historic Park. The park's units include Fort Rosalie, an eighteenth-century fortification. Built by the French, it was occupied by the British, Spanish, and Americans. The William Johnson House was the home and business site owned by a free African-American man.

Hostesses dressed in period costumes escort visitors through the Natchez estates during the spring and fall pilgrimages.

Melrose was the estate of John McMurran, a lawyer who rose to wealth and power.

When you visit Natchez, history surrounds you. It is possible to imagine the city as it was when it was the southern anchor of the Natchez Trace.

SOURCE DOCUMENT

THE RIVER FRONT HERE IS THRONGED WITH BOATS FROM [THROUGHOUT THE] WEST. GREAT QUANTITIES OF FLOUR AND PRODUCE CONTINUALLY PASS. COTTON, THE STAPLE OF THIS TERRITORY, HAS BEEN VERY PRODUCTIVE AND REMUNERATIVE. I HAVE HEARD IT SUGGESTED BY OUR BUSINESS MEN THAT THE AGGREGATE SALES THIS SEASON WILL EXCEED $700,000, A LARGE REVENUE FOR A PEOPLE WHOSE NUMBERS ARE ABOUT 9,000 OF ALL AGES AND COLORS. LABOR IS MORE VALUABLE HERE THAN ELSEWHERE IN THE UNITED STATES, AND INDUSTRIOUS PEOPLE SOON AMASS WEALTH.[10]

The Governor of the Mississippi Territory, William C. Claiborne, reported to Secretary of State James Madison on what he observed at Natchez in the early 1800s.

When the French colonized Natchez, the future site of Nashville was largely an unpopulated wilderness. The region was a hunting ground for American Indians and a few French trappers and traders. The first white settlers did not reach the Cumberland River valley until 1779. For a period in the early 1700s, the site of Nashville was occupied by a group of Shawnee.

NASHVILLE AT THE END OF THE TRACE

A Frenchman briefly set up a trading post among the Shawnee. No one knows his name. People called the area French Lick, because of him and the large salt lick located there.

Around 1769, a second French trader arrived. Jaque-Timothe de Montbrun came to French Lick from Kaskasia, Indiana. There he bought furs from the Indians, and once a year he took his furs down the rivers to sell in New Orleans. By the 1780s, Montbrun had settled at French Lick permanently. He later operated a store and tavern on the town square. In 1769 and again in 1779, long-hunters—explorers from North Carolina and Virginia—hunted in the region for months at a time. When the hunters returned to the eastern settlements, they brought tales of the rich lands and vast animal herds in Central Tennessee.

Richard Henderson Acquires a Claim

In the late 1760s, Virginia and North Carolina were becoming crowded. Settlers began to think of moving farther west. In 1768, Watagua became the first white settlement in East Tennessee. In 1775, North Carolina attorney Richard Henderson was president of the Transylvania Land Company. That spring he met with Cherokee leaders near Watagua. He persuaded them to trade the land between the Cumberland and Ohio rivers to him. In return, he gave the Cherokee a few wagon loads of guns, ammunition, rum, and other goods. Henderson hired Daniel Boone to build a road through the Cumberland Gap to provide access to his holdings.

The British government, the Chickasaw, and officials in Virginia and North Carolina all disputed Henderson's claim. In 1779, Henderson made arrangements for an advance party to scout the Nashville area. He sent thirty-five-year-old James Robertson to find a suitable area for a settlement. Robertson had wide experience on the frontier. He was a farmer, explorer, and surveyor. He had negotiated with the Chickasaw and Cherokee. He and eight scouts made their way west from Watagua. Henderson instructed them to stake out a town site. They were to plant a corn crop to sustain those who would follow.

Robertson chose the area near French Lick, naming it the Bluffs.

Some of Henderson's party returned to Watagua and painted a rosy picture of their new settlement. The scouts told of the great river, the fertile land, and the plentiful supply of fish. They bragged about the large numbers of buffalo and other game that came to the salt lick. The supply of salt was also useful in preserving their meat.

Settlers Come to the Nashville Area

Many in Watagua decided to move to the Bluffs. They came in two parties. The men and boys came on foot, led by Robertson. The first group, a few hundred strong, followed three hundred to four hundred miles of buffalo trails. Despite bitter cold and heavy snows, everyone arrived safely at the Cumberland River. It was Christmas Day, 1779. The river was frozen so they walked across with their livestock. They set up their village on the south bank, knowing they were in danger of attack by the Indians who claimed the land. On the banks of the Cumberland River they quickly erected a stockade, called Fort Nashborough. The name honored Francis Nash, a North Carolina patriot killed during the Revolutionary War.

Two hundred women, children, and elderly men left Watagua on December 22. They formed a thirty-three-boat flotilla. John Donelson led the group from his flatboat, *Adventure*. With him was his tenth child (of eleven), thirteen-year-old Rachel, who would later marry President Andrew Jackson. Severe weather forced the flotilla to stop after going only five miles. After a two-month delay, they restarted the one thousand-mile trip. They traveled down the Holston, down the Tennessee, up the Ohio, and up the Cumberland Rivers. Indian attacks and smallpox claimed many lives. They reached Fort Nashborough on April 24, 1780. The settlers claimed land and built clusters of cabins.

The following month, 256 men from the settlement signed the Cumberland Compact.[1] The document spelled out the system of government and rights of the settlers. Representatives from all the settlements were to meet periodically at the fort. They would provide for the common defense, punish crime, and suppress vice. Only one signer had to sign his name with an X. Under the Compact, James Robertson became the chief civil and military officer. His wise leadership was largely responsible for the settlers' survival.

In April 1781, a coalition of Cherokee, Shawnee, Delaware, and Pottawatomie attacked the fort. In this Battle of the Bluffs, they killed many settlers, then retreated. James Robertson led twenty mounted settlers in pursuit. About the same number of attackers waited in ambush. Robertson's wife released fifty dogs from the fort.[2] In the confusion, Robertson got his force back inside the fort.[3] The attackers left the area. Nevertheless, many of the settlers moved to safer areas.

North Carolina Creates the Town of Nashville

By 1783, no one honored Henderson's land claims. North Carolina organized the area around Nashville as Davidson County. The state allowed 640 acres per person to those remaining on the frontier. It did the same for the heirs of those killed by American Indians. The county court took over day-to-day rule. The judges of the court received their appointments from the state. They licensed a ferry across the Cumberland River and set its rates. They also set the rates for the millers who ground the settlers' corn. In 1784, the North Carolina legislature established the town of Nashville. It set aside two hundred acres near the salt lick to provide land for the construction of the town of six hundred people. There were 165 tree-covered one-acre squares. Four acres were left open for public use, a courthouse and a jail. As a condition of sale, each buyer agreed to build a log building at least sixteen feet square.

Only fifty-three buyers recorded their town lots by 1785. That year Nashville boasted its first school, the Davidson Academy. John Sappington became the settlement's first doctor. There was only one store, owned by Lardner Clark. He arrived in Nashville with ten pack horses loaded with goods. His customers traded corn, tobacco, and pelts for woolen goods, unbleached linen, and calico cloth. Once a year, Clark obtained more goods from Philadelphia. In 1788, Bob Renfroe, a free African-American, opened a popular tavern.

Andrew Jackson came to the settlements on the Cumberland River in October of that year. The young lawyer was only twenty-one. He brought with him a satchel of law books, a slave, and little else. Jackson arrived with a friend, Judge John McNairy. The judge was to serve on the newly created Supreme Court. Jackson agreed to serve as the town's public prosecutor. Jackson boarded at the home of John Donelson's widow. Donelson died in an ambush in 1786 on the trail between Tennessee and Nashville. It was in Donelson's home that Jackson met Rachel Donelson, his future wife. At the time, she was married, but separated from her husband. Nashville kept Jackson busy. Between 1790 and 1794, he worked on over seven hundred cases. Most of the cases involved settlement of debts.[4] Jackson was elected to the House of Representatives in 1796, to the U.S. Senate in 1797, and to the Tennessee Supreme Court in 1798.

Nashville Grows Slowly

In 1790, North Carolina ceded its claims to Tennessee to the United States federal government, allowing Tennessee to become a territory. In 1796, Tennessee became the nation's sixteenth state. In Nashville, Methodists erected the town's first church, located on the public square. Near it were the public stocks, courthouse, and jail. The town's first newspaper started a year later. Almost all businesses centered about the town square. They included the Nashville Inn, the City Hotel, and Talbot's Hotel. The taverns were the largest

Before its incorporation as a town in 1806, the census of 1800 counted only 345 residents of the Nashville area. Today, the nighttime skyline of modern-day Nashville emphasizes its status as the commercial hub of the region.

buildings in the city. Talbot's boasted nine rooms and twenty-three windows. The log structures included warehouses, lawyers' offices, artisans' sheds, and a Masonic hall.

Nashville was not growing rapidly. The census of 1800 listed only 345 people. Almost half of them were slaves. The population was very young. Of the 191 whites, only twelve men were over forty-five. Only a hundred men and thirty-five women were over the age of sixteen.[5] Nashville did not incorporate itself as a town until 1806. It then elected a mayor and six aldermen to govern the town. That year, Cumberland College incorporated itself, serving as a successor to the Davidson Academy. Many years later, it became the University of Nashville.

Volunteers formed a fire-fighting force in 1807. Former vice president Aaron Burr traveled through Nashville. The town gained its first bank, the Bank of Nashville. A publishing firm published its first book three years later. The state legislature met in Nashville for the first time in 1812. (The city did not become Tennessee's permanent capital until 1843). By this time, roughly twelve hundred people called Nashville home.

Nashville saw much activity along the Natchez Trace during the War of 1812 (1812–15). In 1818, the first steamboat, the *Andrew Jackson*, arrived in Nashville. It signaled a rapid decline for the Natchez Trace. By this time, Nashville had established its own importance. The city continued to grow long after the Natchez Trace slipped into history. James Monroe made the first presidential visit to the town in 1819. A stone bridge spanned the Cumberland River three years later.

★ NEWLYWED ANDREW JACKSON TRAVELS THE TRACE ★

Andrew Jackson was only twenty-three when he first traveled the trace. In the summer of 1790 he bought a tract of land twenty-five miles north of Natchez. He built a log house, and talked about building a racecourse. He

In 1791, recently married Rachel Jackson traveled on horseback from Natchez to Nashville along the Trace.

returned to Nashville via the Natchez Trace.

Early in 1791, Jackson accompanied his wife-to-be, Rachel Robards, by flatboat to Natchez. Rachel Donelson had married Lewis Robards in 1785, when she was seventeen. Robards claimed Rachel had an affair with Peyton Short, a lawyer, who was a boarder in the Robards house. Robards sent Rachel home to her widowed mother. They lived ten miles south of Nashville.

In the spring of 1790, Rachel and Robards reconciled briefly. They went together to Kentucky. In July, at the request of her family, Jackson went to bring Rachel back to Nashville. Robards followed her there, seeking another reconciliation. The family decided Rachel would be safer in Natchez.[6] Jackson delivered her to Springfield Plantation, the home of Thomas Green, a family friend. His mission completed, Jackson returned up the Trace to Nashville.

A few months later, Jackson heard that the Robards were divorced, so he rushed to Natchez. In August 1791, Andrew Jackson married Rachel Donelson Robards. Within a month, the newlyweds were traveling north to Nashville. The Jacksons were part of a company of one hundred persons. Travel in large companies was a standard safety practice on the Natchez Trace. It is probable that African-American slaves accompanied them on the three-week trip. Jackson and his wife rode on horseback. At that time, there were no inns along the way. The Jacksons spent their nights in a tent under the stars.

The trail was thick with dust, and the party sometimes had to skirt swamps swarming with mosquitoes and gnats. In late summer, the streams were not swollen. Horses could wade across most of the larger ones, while rafts carried their luggage and goods across. Smaller streams often were bridged by a fallen tree. The

When Rachel and Andrew Jackson arrived in Nashville 1791, they built their home, the Hermitage.

SOURCE DOCUMENT

"ALL YOUNG MEN OVER THE AGE OF SIXTEEN YEARS AND ABLE TO PERFORM MILITIA DUTY SHALL BE CONSIDERED AS HAVING A FULL RIGHT TO ENTER FOR AND OBTAIN LANDS IN THEIR OWN NAME AS IF THEY WERE OF FULL AGE AND IN THAT CASE NOT BE RECKONED IN THE FAMILY OF THE FATHER, MOTHER, OR MASTER SO AS TO AVAIL THEM OF ANY LAND ON THEIR ACCOUNT.

WHERE ANY PERSON SHALL MARK OF IMPROVE LAND OR LANDS WITH INTENT TO SET UP A CLAIM THERETO, SUCH PERSON SHALL WRITE OR MARK IN LEGIBLE CHARACTERS THE INITIAL LETTERS OF HIS NAME AT LEAST, TOGETHER WITH THE DAY OF THE MONTH AND YEAR ON WHICH HE MARKED OR IMPROVED THE SAME AT THE SPRING OR MOST NOTORIOUS PART OF THE LAND OR ON SOME CONVENIENT TREE, OR OTHER DURABLE SUBSTANCE, IN ORDER TO NOTIFY HIS INTENTIONS TO ALL SUCH AS MAY INQUIRE OR EXAMINE.[7]

The Pilgrims arrived at Plymouth, Massachusetts in 1620. They promptly organized a government in the Mayflower Compact. Over 150 years later, the settlers at Nashville did the same. This excerpt from their Cumberland Compact shows their concern over land titles.

swift-flowing Tennessee River was the biggest obstacle. Its banks were lined by walls of tall canes. At the best crossing point, it was a quarter-mile wide.

The Jacksons lived near Nashville in a home called the Hermitage. In 1793, Jackson learned that Rachel's divorce from Robards had never been finalized. A divorce decree was issued that year, and Rachel and Andrew Jackson remarried in 1794.

6

HAZARDS OF THE NATCHEZ TRACE

Travel along the Natchez Trace was perilous at best. Hazards encountered on the Trace came from both natural and human sources.

Natural Hazards

For much of the route, the terrain was inhospitable. The Trace went through swamps that were almost impassable. Water was deep at some points, and travelers had to swim to cross them. In the swamps, mire sometimes came up to the saddle skirts of a rider on horseback. Beneath the mud, the bottom was thick clay. Horses could become hopelessly stuck. There was no option but to shoot them or abandon them to a slow death. Earthquakes and tornadoes tore up the woodlands, and fallen trees obliterated miles of trail. Travelers had to grope their way through impenetrable thickets until they found the Trace again. High winds and floods sometimes made rivers uncrossable. In winter, bitter cold brought with it sleet and snow.

Travelers heard tales of attacks by bands of wild animals. To be sure, there were bears and wolves in the forests, but these accounts were largely fictional. Veterans of the Trace enjoyed telling them to frighten

The winter months often brought snow to the Natchez Trace.
Even though the snow rarely stayed on the ground for long,
the bitter cold hindered travelers.

first time travelers. This did not stop people from keeping blazing fires going at night to frighten animals away.

People fell victim to many illnesses along the Trace. Drinking impure water was one of the primary causes. Poison ivy caused swelling and itching on exposed arms and legs. During wet weather, insect bites brought severe discomfort. Not all hazards came from nature. Outlaws added to the hazards of the Trace.

Samuel Mason Becomes an Outlaw

Samuel Mason was the most notorious robber of the Natchez Trace. He was born in Virginia about 1739. Mason was a tall man and weighed about two hundred pounds. One tooth projected forward. He had a large hooked nose. He was a powerful and persuasive talker. During the Revolutionary War, he served as a militia captain under George Rogers Clark. His career in crime spanned almost a half century. In the 1760s, he stole horses in what is now eastern West Virginia. A decade later he stole supplies from Fort Henry near Wheeling. In the 1780s, he ran up debts in West Virginia's Washington County. In July 1781, Mason won election as a Justice of the Peace. A month later he was named an associate judge. Mason was married, with four daughters and six sons.

In 1794, Mason is suspected to have killed a tavern owner. He left West Virginia, relocating to a noted robber's roost, the "Cave In Rock" on the Ohio River. He set up a store and pretended to sell goods to passing flatboat crews. When they landed their boats, Mason and his gang robbed the boatmen. Legend says that the robbers beat their victims and left them for dead. Mason and his gang then took the flatboats down the river to New Orleans. There they sold the vessels and their cargo. The fame of Mason's gang grew. Soon every robbery on the Ohio and Mississippi was blamed on them. In 1799, citizens organized a group of flatboats at Pittsburgh to attack Mason's stronghold. Mason learned of their plans, and his gang fled and separated. Mason relocated briefly to Wolf Island in the Mississippi. In 1800, he appeared at New Madrid in Spanish-ruled Missouri. He was successful in obtaining a Spanish passport there.

Mason Moves to the Natchez Trace

Mason gave up attacking boats. It was easier to lie in wait on the trails. He and his gang stole from travelers, taking the proceeds they carried after selling their boats and their cargo. Mason's career as a thief and murderer on the Natchez Trace began in 1801. At this time, his gang consisted of his sons Mango and Thomas, Mason's brother John, Thomas Setton, Wiley Harpe, and six or so others. Accompanying them were a number of women and at least three children. Mason settled near Rocky Springs, forty miles north of Natchez. Some of the gang remained in or near Natchez. Others remained in New Madrid and Bayou Pierre. They kept an eye out for northbound travelers who seemed to have money.

During his years as an infamous bandit, Samuel Mason settled near Rocky Springs. Today, little remains of the small settlement.

Colonel Joshua Baker had a good year in 1801. The Kentucky planter had sailed to New Orleans with a year's goods. It took several flatboats to contain his livestock and produce. On the return trip, he and three others rode up the Trace. Their five pack horses carried provisions and buckskin bags of gold. When they stopped for their midday rest at Twelve-Mile Creek, they were ninety miles up the Trace. Mason and his gang successfully robbed the party of their riding horses and most of their money.

The news of the robbery spread up and down the Trace. At either end of the Trace, travelers waited until they could join a large group. On the trail, men passed each other warily. They scanned each other's faces, seeking a clue as to intent. Mason himself sometimes stopped John Swaney, the mail carrier. Mason was anxious to know what was said of him. He asked Swaney for news and events from each end of the Trace. The outlaw and mail carrier chatted in peace by the side of the trail.

One night on the Trace, Swaney witnessed a murder. He awoke an hour before daybreak. Riding at a fast clip, he heard voices ahead. Swaney blew his trumpet to announce his coming. He hoped to get some food in return for giving the travelers his news. Swaney heard a shout, and then a shot. Ahead, he saw a mounted traveler. Near him was a robber on foot, his musket raised. The robber wore war paint as a disguise. The robber fired. The traveler, a Georgian named Robert McAlpin, fell. Coolly, the robber darted into the cane beside the trail. Swaney rode for help to Pigeon Roost, a nearby settlement. On the way, Swaney caught up with two fleeing riders. They were McAlpin's son and a friend. When they returned, they found McAlpin's body stripped to the underwear. His horse and the money in his saddlebags were also gone.[1]

The End of Mason

One day, Mason and his son rode down the Trace to Natchez. Mason had a friend there named Anthony Glass. Glass had the reputation of being an honest merchant, but he was actually Mason's agent. Glass sent word ahead when a rich prize was heading up the Trace. Glass resold the items Mason and his gang stole.

In Natchez a passerby recognized Mason. Arrested, Mason and his son found themselves in the stone Spanish jail. Mason faced trial for robbing Colonel Baker. The jurors found him guilty, and Mason was sentenced to a thirty-nine lash public whipping. Afterward, he was locked by the neck and wrists in the public pillory for twelve hours. Throughout the trial and punishment, Mason proclaimed himself innocent.

Mason did not reappear in Natchez for a long while. The robberies and murders on the Trace continued. Mason's successes infuriated the governor of the Mississippi Territory, William Claiborne. The governor sent troops up and down the Trace looking for Mason, without any success. Claiborne offered a reward of $2,000 for Mason's capture.[2] A raiding party invaded Mason's camp, but found it deserted. They began to dig for the treasure rumored to be buried there, but found none. People still seek Mason's gold in the region's swampy ground.

Mason had moved back to the Mississippi and set up headquarters on Stack Island, fifty miles north of Vicksburg, Mississippi. In January 1803, Mason rented a house near New Madrid. Spanish authorities arrested Mason and most of his gang and sent them to New Orleans. The authorities there decided to turn them over to the Americans. Coming upriver, the gang escaped, and for six months Mason eluded capture. Then Claiborne's reward offer paid off. Two of Mason's men, Wiley Harpe and James Mays, were alone with him. They killed him with a tomahawk blow, cut off his head, and encased the head in a lumpy ball of blue clay. They brought it to Natchez to collect the reward. Instead, local citizens identified them as gang members. They were tried and executed, and their own heads were cut off and mounted on poles along the Trace as a warning to other would-be robbers.[3]

With Mason's gang removed, the worst was over. Even during his prime, there were only half a dozen murders on the Trace. Isolated robberies continued. Travelers on the Trace continued to see one or two riders following them at a distance, sometimes for hours. They might be innocent of any harmful intent, or they might be looking for a good place to attack. At night, travelers hid in the woods, often concealing their valuables, tying them to trees away from their campsites.

Some robbers posed as Methodist ministers to gain their victims' trust. One of them, James Copeland, bragged that he spent days teaching his henchmen to pray and say "Amen!"[4]

Many legends grew up around the Land Pirates of the Natchez Trace. The supposed number of their crimes increased as time passed. Legend said John Murrell was the greatest of them all. People said Murrell killed four hundred people. They believed that he led a thousand robbers. In reality, he was a small-time thief. At age seventeen, he went to prison for stealing a horse. From then on, Murrell was in and out of jail. He died of tuberculosis at age thirty-eight.

On the Trace, natural hazards and the threat of robbers were real enough. They naturally attracted those who enjoyed spinning dark tales. Virgil A. Stewart had a vivid imagination. He wrote in a small pamphlet about wholesale crime on the Natchez Trace. He portrayed the Trace as one of the most evil places on earth. That portrait was not 100 percent wrong.

★ A Mysterious Death on the Natchez Trace ★

Meriwether Lewis was a leader of the famous Lewis and Clark expedition. Earlier, he was President Thomas Jefferson's private secretary. From 1804 through 1806, Lewis explored the recently acquired Louisiana Purchase. Jefferson rewarded Lewis by naming him governor of the vast territory of Louisiana.

Lewis took office in March 1808, but he did not do well. He disliked the daily details of government.

WE ARE INFORMED THAT ON THE FOURTEENTH OF AUGUST, ABOUT SIXTY MILES ON THIS SIDE OF THE BIG BIOPIERE RIVER, COLONEL JOSHUA BAKER, A MR. WILLIAM BAKER AND A MR. ROGERS OF NATCHEZ, WERE ROBBED OF THEIR HORSES, TRAVELING UTENSILS, AND ABOUT $2,300 CASH.

IT SEEMS THE COMPANY HAD HALTED IN THE MORNING AT A SMALL CLEAR STREAM OF WATER IN ORDER TO WASH. AS SOON AS THEY HAD DISMOUNTED AND GONE TO THE WATER, FOUR MEN APPEARED, BLACKED, BETWEEN THEM AND THEIR HORSES, AND DEMANDED SURRENDER OF THEIR MONEY AND PROPERTY, WHICH THEY WERE OBLIGED TO COMPLY WITH.

MR. W. BAKER WAS MORE FORTUNATE THAN HIS COMPANIONS. A PACK-HORSE, ON WHICH WAS A CONSIDERABLE SUM OF MONEY, BEING FRIGHTENED AT THE APPEARANCE OF THE ROBBERS, RAN AWAY, AND THEY BEING IN HASTE TO ESCAPE COULD NOT PURSUE. MR. BAKER RECOVERED HIS HORSE AND MONEY. HE, HOWEVER, LOST HIS RIDING HORSE, ETC.

COLONEL BAKER AND MR. ROGERS CAME TO THE FIRST SETTLEMENT, WHERE THEY PROCURED ASSISTANCE AND IMMEDIATELY WENT IN PURSUIT OF THE VILLAINS. IT IS TO BE HOPED THEY WILL BE APPREHENDED.[5]

A contemporary newspaper account of the activities of Samuel Mason on the Natchez Trace.

Squabbling officeholders made governing difficult. Lewis invested unwisely in land, losing heavily. Without authority, he spent thousands of dollars in government funds. Knowing his reputation was at stake, Lewis decided to go to Washington, D.C. There he would try to clear his name.

Lewis sold everything he had to pay his debts. On September 4, 1809, Lewis left St. Louis. He went by ship

A monument marks the burial site of the famed explorer Meriwether Lewis. As part of the famed Lewis and Clark expedition, he explored the newly-purchased Louisiana territory between 1804 and 1806. He was then appointed as the region's first governor.

down the Mississippi River, planning to go to New Orleans. From there, he would go by ship to Washington. On reaching Fort Pickering (today's Memphis, Tennessee), he changed his plans. He decided to ride east to the Natchez Trace, then follow it to Nashville. From there he would continue his journey overland.

His problems still weighed on him, and he appeared to be mentally ill. The commander of Fort Pickering took Lewis into his home to rest for a few days. He feared that Lewis might commit suicide, but the rest seemed to help.[6] On September 29, Lewis left the fort along with Major James Neely and two servants. Nine days later, they reached the Tennessee River and headed up the Natchez Trace.

On October 10, two of their horses ran away. Neely went after the horses while Lewis and the servants went to an inn along the Trace known as the Grinder's Stand, at sunset. Lewis asked the innkeeper's wife for food and whiskey. He did not eat or drink much. He obtained some gunpowder from her. She left to sleep in another building. The servants slept in a barn, and Lewis was alone. The innkeeper's wife later reported hearing him talking loudly to someone. Then witnesses reported hearing two or three shots ring out. The servants found Lewis lying on the floor. He had a wound in the chest and in the head. His two pistols were at his side. It looked as though he had taken his own life.

Rumors began to circulate. Some said the innkeeper had returned and tried to rob Lewis. Others said the servants were involved in Lewis's death. Some reports mentioned knife wounds. How did Meriwether Lewis really die? The debate over whether it was suicide or murder continues today.

7

THE FINAL YEARS OF THE NATCHEZ TRACE

By 1800, there were no European troops along the Natchez Trace. The British had left the area over a decade earlier. The Spanish sailed south to New Orleans a few years before 1800. But there were both British and Spanish agents on the trail. The activities of the agents covered the whole Trace. Even the American military commander, General James Wilkinson, was on the Spanish payroll. The foreign agents had a goal. They encouraged the area's residents to break loose from the United States. That would make it easier for a European power to reclaim the area. In 1803, Napoleon ruled France. Napoleon feared the British would take the Mississippi Valley by force. Instead, he sold the Louisiana Territory to the United States.

President Thomas Jefferson was worried. He was not sure Spain would go along with the deal. The Spanish in New Orleans had no inkling of the change in ownership. Jefferson decided to have American troops ready to enforce the exchange. He sent orders to the Mississippi Territory to turn out the militia. A request from the president for five hundred mounted troopers arrived in West Tennessee. Tennessee governor John Sevier promised to send them down the Natchez Trace at once.

American Troops March Down the Natchez Trace

In the past, Indian war parties had traveled the Natchez Trace. Now it would be a military road again. The Tennessee troopers headed south in early December 1803. They rode in single file down the trail. Their trip took three weeks. Upon reaching Washington, Mississippi, they had startling news. Their trip had been for nothing. The Spanish had turned New Orleans over to Governor Claiborne and General Wilkinson without trouble. Many of the young riders were disappointed. They were anxious to see some action. Natchez threw a festive dinner for the visiting officers. Then the Tennessee troops returned home up the Trace, arriving in Nashville a few weeks later. They were covered with trail dust, not glory.[1]

A decade later, troops again headed down the Natchez Trace toward New Orleans. Britain was at war with France, while the United States remained neutral. Ignoring the neutral status, the British were stopping and searching American ships on the high seas looking for goods on the way to France. They confiscated those they found. The British also forced some sailors on American ships to join the British navy. The United

States declared war on Great Britain, signaling the beginning of the War of 1812.

The war did not go well for the United States. British agents encouraged the Shawnee chief Tecumseh to drive settlers from the Northwest. The British repulsed American efforts to invade Canada. Everyone expected the British to move into the Gulf and attack New Orleans.

Jackson's Troops Serve in Vain

Andrew Jackson raised twenty-five hundred volunteers. He told them, "Every man in the Western Country turns his eyes intuitively upon the mouth of the Mississippi. To the people of the Western Country is then peculiarly committed by nature herself the defense of the lower Mississippi."[2] Jackson moved at once, sending 670 mounted horsemen down the Natchez Trace. He led a force of 1,830 volunteers on flatboats. They would go down the Cumberland River to the Ohio River. The flatboats would follow the Ohio to its juncture with the Mississippi. The current would carry them downstream toward New Orleans. One obstacle was that the winter of 1813 was brutally harsh. There was a possibility the rivers could freeze over, trapping Jackson's flatboats.

Colonel John Coffee led the mounted troops down the Natchez Trace on January 19, 1813. It took his force six days just to reach the Tennessee River. He spent two more days at the river ferry. The men and animals crossed in freezing weather. The ferry-keeper,

George Colbert, charged high fees for ferrying and feeding the troops. South of the river, the troops traveled twenty to twenty-three miles a day. Coffee got word from travelers coming up the Trace that British troops had yet to appear at New Orleans. This discouraged the men, since they did not want a repeat of the 1803 false alarm. Two weeks into the trip, the riders reached the Chickasaw villages, where American Indians brought them food.

Almost two weeks later, on February 16, 1813, the mounted men reached Natchez. That same day, Jackson and his flatboats arrived at Natchez-Under-The-Hill. Jackson was upset that his intended campsite, Fort Dearborn, was in disrepair. Its houses were rotting. Jackson had his entire force camp on a plain west of Washington, Mississippi, only a few miles from Natchez. The army waited for orders from General Wilkinson. Jackson's men fretted—they had enlisted to fight—but now they were sitting in the snow in Mississippi. A month passed, and then on March 22, orders came. Jackson was to march his whole force back to Nashville over the Trace. No pay was provided for the troops. They had no wagons for their sick. Jackson paid for thirteen wagons and twenty-six pack horses from his own money.[3]

Jackson's force moved north as he walked with the troops. He let those who were ill use his horse. The men admired the way he shared their hardships. They gave him the nickname Old Hickory for his toughness. His march began on March 25, and his troops reached

Nashville four weeks later. They received a hero's welcome. The local politicians and newspapers praised them. In the public square, Nashville's ladies presented the troops with rich flags. Then the troops went quietly to their homes.

Andrew Jackson Saves New Orleans

In 1814, the British invaded and burned public buildings in Washington, D.C. British and American commissioners began talking peace at Ghent, Belgium, that summer. Meanwhile, the British defeated the French emperor Napoleon in 1814, and were free to concentrate their efforts on the American war. A fleet of over fifty British warships appeared in the Gulf of

Mexico carrying thousands of soldiers. Their obvious target was New Orleans. It was going to be a race. When would British lieutenant general Sir Edward Pakenham attack New Orleans?

Andrew Jackson frequently traveled on the Natchez Trace. During the War of 1812, American troops traveled the trail, repeatedly going between Nashville and New Orleans.

Would there be enough American troops there in time to defend the city?

In December, Jackson organized his defenses. This time most of his troops came to New Orleans by water rather than down the Trace. Major General John Thomas led twenty-three hundred Kentucky Militia. Thomas reported on December 8 that his troops would need twenty to twenty-five days to get to New Orleans. Major General William Carroll arrived in Natchez on December 13 with three thousand Tennessee volunteers. Thomas Hinds was en route with 107 Mississippi Mounted Dragoons; heavily armed soldiers on horseback. John Coffee arrived on the December 20 with eight hundred mounted soldiers.

The British landed safely seven miles from New Orleans, but could not attack at once. By December 25, the British army was fully drawn up below the city. Jackson faced them with a battle line between the Mississippi and a swamp. For days, the British erected gun positions opposite Jackson's lines. The new year began with an artillery duel that decided nothing. The British made a frontal assault on January 8. American sharpshooters fired at massed ranks from behind their mud wall. Over two thousand British were killed or wounded. Among the dead was General Pakenham. The Americans lost thirteen soldiers.[4] The British retreated to their ships. Jackson had saved New Orleans.

The Battle of New Orleans need never have taken place. A peace treaty between Britain and the United States was signed on Christmas Eve, two weeks before the battle. News of the signing did not reach the United States until February 1815. Natchez received the word in March.

The victorious troops marched northward to Natchez. Then they headed up the Trace. Reverend John G. Jones wrote:

> For many months [I] had often seen soldiers marching southward. But now they were marching with light step and merry heart, in the opposite direction. First came a heavy brigade of Tennessee infantry. Then came regiments of mounted riflemen and squadrons of light dragoons of various size. These were followed by smaller detachments of both infantry and cavalry. Last came the sick and their attendants. For months we seldom looked up or down the Natchez Trace without seeing passing soldiers.[5]

Jackson stayed in New Orleans until April 6, 1815. His wife, Rachel, came by flatboat to join him. It was her first visit to a city larger than Nashville. The Jacksons' return to Nashville was a triumphal march. They reached Natchez on April 20. Natchez had suffered economically during the war because the British had blocked cotton exports. For three years, the Mississippi River had flooded low-lying fields, and as a result Natchez was at its most beautiful. The city decorated itself with lights, then held a ball in Jackson's honor. Rachel Jackson wore a silk dress trimmed with lace, a gift from the people of New Orleans.

Celebrations continued as the Jacksons moved up the Natchez Trace. Ovations occurred in Washington, Selsertown, and Greenville. Road conditions had improved since Jackson and his bride first rode the Trace, but it was still a bumpy ride. The general and his wife rode in a carriage, and stayed at some of the a dozen or so roadside inns, called stands. They were not as comfortable as the hotels in Nashville or Natchez. Still, staying at the stands was better than spending the nights under the stars. Hundreds of ill and wounded troops saw the Jacksons pass. They had left their units along the Trace. Many of the soldiers received care at the stands and from the Choctaw and Chickasaw. Legend has it that the ferryman at the Tennessee crossing collected $75,000 to ferry Jackson's army across.

Two developments soon spelled the end of the Natchez Trace. More and more steamboats plied the western rivers. In 1820, a new road system extended from Nashville to New Orleans. Named Andrew Jackson's Military Highway, the road shortened the route by 220 miles.

★ A STEAMBOAT SIGNALS THE END OF THE NATCHEZ TRACE ★

Robert Fulton's steamboat *Clermont* made its first trip up the Hudson River in 1807. Two weeks later, he turned his attention to the west. Fulton obtained a monopoly on steamboat travel on the Mississippi River. In 1809, Fulton's firm sent Nicholas Roosevelt to Pittsburgh to survey the western rivers. (Nicholas Roosevelt was the brother of President Theodore Roosevelt's great-grandfather.) He and his wife, Lydia, floated downstream on a flatboat, and then upstream on a steamboat. Westerners laughed at the idea of a boat that could travel upstream. Nevertheless, Roosevelt's report was favorable. In September 1811, the firm launched the *New Orleans* from a shipyard near Pittsburgh.

The *New Orleans* cost $38,000. The steamship was 20 feet wide and 148 feet long. Its engine produced less than a hundred horsepower. Side-wheels propelled the ship through the water.[6] On its maiden voyage, the ship carried Roosevelt, his wife, the captain, an engineer, a river pilot, six deckhands, two servants, a cook, and a Newfoundland dog. For the first two days, the ship went downstream at a speed of eight to ten miles an hour. In Cincinnati, the mayor told Roosevelt, "We see you for the last time. Your boat may go *down* the river, but as to coming up, the very idea is absurd."[7]

In Louisville, the ship's steam whistle terrified the citizens. Roosevelt put on a demonstration for the riverbank crowd. He invited guests on board, taking them upstream a few miles.[8] Once past Louisville, the ship ran into a series of difficulties. Low water in the Ohio caused a delay in passing through the falls of the Ohio River. A major earthquake rocked the boat severely. The *New Orleans* easily outran Chickasaw warriors pursuing them in a canoe. Another night, the ship caught fire, destroying the forward cabin.

Thousands of onlookers welcomed the *New Orleans* to Natchez. At that moment, the ship lost power and started drifting downstream. Just in time, the engineer restored power. The *New Orleans* docked safely. It then made its way safely to its namesake city. Roosevelt began steamboat service between the city of New Orleans and

Natchez. The ten to twenty upstream passengers paid $30 each.[9] The *New Orleans* hit a snag and sank in 1814. The following year the steamboat *Enterprise* made the return trip all the way to Louisville. By the end of 1817, nine steamboats plied the western rivers. The days of the Natchez Trace were numbered.

Throughout the eighteenth century, the Natchez Trace was very heavily traveled. Over the decades, travelers wore the trail down several feet in places. But by 1817 steamboats controlled the rivers, and the Natchez Trace was soon to be abandoned.

8

TRAVELING THE NATCHEZ TRACE PARKWAY

The Natchez Trace Parkway is a two-lane 450-mile highway. The scenic byway connects Natchez and Nashville. Where possible it follows the route of the historic Trace. The road crosses Mississippi, a corner of Alabama, and Tennessee. The road is open year round for motorists, hikers, and cyclists. The Parkway is maintained by the U.S. Department of the Interior. The Parkway headquarters is in Tupelo, Mississippi.

During the Great Depression of the 1930s, the U.S. government put many unemployed people back to work. It hired many to construct park facilities. Congressman Thomas Jefferson (Jeff) Busby, from Mississippi, introduced a bill for a survey of the Natchez Trace. In 1934, Congress appropriated $50,000 for the survey. President Franklin Roosevelt signed the bill, and the following year, Congress appropriated $1.2 million to begin constructing the Natchez Trace Parkway.

The idea was to provide motorists with uninterrupted travel. Sometimes local roads crossed the

Parkway. The engineers routed them over or under the new road. The Civilian Conservation Corps (CCC) set up work camps for the young men who built it. After rights-of-way were acquired, road grading began. In 1938, 1.5 million more federal dollars followed. That year, Congress included the Natchez Trace Parkway as a part of the National Park Service. Between 1928 and 1941, Congress added another $3.5 million.

Construction stopped during the United States participation in World War II (1941–45). It continued after the war. Today the route is virtually completed. Along the Parkway are over forty-five thousand acres

The two-lane, 450-mile-long Natchez Trace Parkway links Nashville and Natchez. The Parkway offers a scenic drive along much of the old Natchez Trace route.

of federal land. In many sections, the Parkway boundary is no wider than the highway. In others, the property line wanders into the woods for several hundred yards. The Parkway features nature trails, scenic overlooks, historic monuments, and visitor centers. There are fifteen major interpretive locations where a visitor can learn about the park. All along the route are rest rooms and picnic grounds. There are three major campgrounds. From the Parkway, there is easy access to nearby towns. Signposts reveal the historic events that took place at many spots along the Parkway.[1] The markers summarize the entire history of the thoroughfare.

The Park Service works to make it easy to enjoy the natural beauty of the countryside. Commercial traffic is banned, as are billboards and advertising signs. Rights-of-way are often lined with split-rail fences. The natural habitat has been preserved wherever possible. For example, beaver once almost vanished, but have since made a dramatic comeback.

The Southern End of the Parkway

The southern portion winds past gently rolling farmland. In spring, the valleys blaze with yellow wildflowers. Towering cypress rise from still, dank swamps, and white-tailed deer scurry across the road. The Parkway begins seven miles north of Natchez. Less than a mile up the road is the first section of the old Natchez Trace. A mile farther along is the Emerald Mound. It is the second largest Indian mound in the country. The eight-acre mound dates to about A.D. 1300. Visitors can follow a path to the top.

Near milepost 15, Mount Locust is the only "stand" still in existence. The one-room cabin and four room annex were one day's walk from Natchez. Also near the milepost is a road that leads to Springfield Plantation, about a mile away. It was there that Andrew Jackson proposed marriage to Rachel Donelson Robards. Travelers can walk a sunken portion of the original Trace near milepost 46. Moss drips

Rock Spring continues to provide fresh water—just as it has for hundreds of years. During the years when the Natchez Trace was frequented, travelers would camp by springs like Rock Spring. Today it is still an area where tourists of the Trace can camp.

from trailside trees, the undergrowth is tangled, and the chirp of crickets fills the air.

Rocky Springs is the first major campground. Near milepost 55, it also offers picnic tables, rest rooms, and a ranger station. A few miles north was the southern edge of Choctaw lands. There is an intersection with Mississippi Highway 27 at milepost 67. It provides access to the historic city of Vicksburg and its Civil War National Military Park. Twenty miles farther along, the Parkway intersects U.S. Interstate 20. It leads to Jackson, the state capital of Mississippi.

The Mississippi Craft Center is near milepost 102. In the old cabin are items for sale made by Choctaw artisans. From March to October, there are weekend craft demonstrations. For the next twenty miles, the Parkway is paralleled by Cypress Swamp. Near milepost 120, a twenty-minute walk follows a nature trail. The visitor can easily understand why earlier travelers dreaded crossing the area. The first section of the trail is over a raised boardwalk. Turtles abound in the still swamp waters, while herons swoop down to fish. What looks like a drifting log might turn out to be an alligator.

Just north of the swamp the Choctaw lands ended. The Southern third of the Parkway ends near milepost 159. The turnoff to Koscinszko is just above the local ranger station. A museum in the town tells of the Polish nobleman who served with Washington in the Revolutionary War.

A boardwalk built by the National Park Service allows visitors to explore Cypress Swamp. The swamp waters are teeming with turtles, herons, and even the occasional alligator.

The Middle Third of the Parkway

The middle third of the Parkway is also in Mississippi. It begins with two widely different nature trails. The Hurricane Creek trail (milepost 164) proceeds through bottomland to dry hilltops. The short Cole Creek trail (milepost 176), takes hikers through a beautiful swamp. It is lined with bald cypress and water tupelo trees.

At one time, there were thirteen Christian missions to the Choctaw. One of them, Bethel Mission, stood near milepost 176. Here missionaries combined teaching religion with reading, writing, and mathematics. When the Trace fell into disuse, the missions declined. Bethel Mission closed in 1826.

The town of French Camp, near milepost 181, was the home of Louis Le Fleur. In 1812, he, his wife, and children established a stand along the Natchez Trace. Le Fleur's son, Greenwood, became the Choctaw nation's last elected chief. Income from a craft store, museum, and gift shop help to support the French Camp Academy. The school serves children in need of stable home environments.

Jeff Busby is a site named for the congressman who first sponsored the creation of the Parkway. Here at milepost 193 is the only service station on the Parkway. The area also includes a convenience store, telephone, campground, nature trail, and rest rooms.

The Bynum Mounds at milepost 232 are two thousand years old. The Mound Builders erected them during the Woodland Period. They occupied the site between 100 B.C. and A.D. 200. Bodies buried within the mounds wore copper from the Lake Superior region and flint from the Ohio region. On-site exhibits portray the Mound Builders' hunting, farming, and village life. The present-day Parkway may well follow the trade routes of these people

Near milepost 241, the United States maintained an agency for the Chickasaw from 1802 to 1825. These years coincided with the time of heavy traffic on the Natchez Trace. Five miles down the Parkway, at the Monroe Mission, many Chickasaw people first learned about Christianity. Somehow, more than 150 people managed to squeeze into the sixteen-square-foot buildings to be baptized.

The sites of two Chickasaw villages are between mileposts 262 and 264. At Chickasaw Village, visitors can watch a taped presentation showing what Chickasaw life was like in the 1700s. At that time, travelers renamed one Chickasaw village Old Town. It was the scene of their 1795 victory over invading people of the Creek tribe.

The Natchez Trace Parkway Headquarters and Visitor Center is at milepost 266. Friendly rangers are pleased to answer your questions. This is a good place to pick up literature, tapes, and postcards about the Natchez Trace. The bookstore also carries material on the Civil War and local history. Rangers will play a twelve-minute slide presentation upon request. Those interested can make a side trip to nearby Tupelo, birthplace of Elvis Presley.

The Northern End of the Parkway

Only a little more than thirty miles of the Parkway are in Alabama. The Parkway enters the state at milepost 309. The roadway passes through rolling hills. These are the Freedom Hills. They are the southernmost outposts of the Appalachian Mountains. They range in height from four hundred to almost a thousand feet. Pine and oak trees dot their summits.

The site of Colbert's Ferry lies at milepost 327. Crossing the Tennessee River was always a major obstacle on the Natchez Trace. In modern times, Pickwick Dam greatly widened the river at this point. The highway engineers erected the mile-long John Coffee Memorial Bridge. At Colbert's Ferry, there are a ranger station, picnic area, swimming area, fishing area, boat launch, and rest rooms.

The Parkway reaches the Tennessee border at milepost 340. Thirty miles farther north, U.S. Highway 64 runs east to Lawrenceburg. The area is closely associated with Davy Crockett. Crockett arrived in 1816, and the famed frontiersman served as a justice of the peace, state assemblyman, and U.S. congressman. One block south of the town square is the David Crockett Cabin and Museum. Nearby is David Crockett State Park. Here Crockett once operated a grist mill, distillery, and powder mill.

It is possible near milepost 376 to drive along a 2.5-mile section of the old trace. The one-way drive is not suitable for those with trailers, but it is not necessary to have a four-wheel-drive vehicle. The unpaved drive has tight turns. There is a shallow ford across a stream. Springtime brings out the dogwood and azaleas. In fall, the leaves are a riot of color.

Napier Mine, near milepost 382, is a huge pit. Here workers dug rich iron ore. They dragged huge chunks to an area where they were broken into smaller chunks. These they loaded onto wagons to take to the ironworks nearby. At nearby Metal Ford, Steels Iron Works began smelting iron in 1820. The charcoal-burning process used water from the nearby Buffalo River.

When Steels Iron Works opened in 1820, water from the Buffalo River was used in the smelting process of iron ore.

Markers tell the story of Meriwether Lewis's mysterious death at milepost 385. The Tobacco Barn at milepost 401 is of an early-twentieth-century date. In the facility, tobacco dried after harvest. Tennessee is the third largest tobacco-growing state, and it is the state's biggest cash crop.

Near milepost 426, there is a twenty-minute hike along a section of the Natchez Trace. The section was first cleared by the U.S. Army in 1901. It is the last such section open before the Parkway's end. For most, Garrison Creek is the last stop before reaching busy Tennessee highways near Nashville. The facility at milepost 437 is a trailhead for hikers and horseback riders. The name Garrison Creek comes from the army unit stationed here in 1808.

How much time does it take to travel the Natchez Trace Parkway? There is no one answer. It depends on the wishes and interests of each traveler. If time is short, a traveler can do one section thoroughly. Heading north, one can spend the first night in Kosciuszko. Tupelo is a possible second-night stop, and Nashville is a good place to stay near the Parkway's end. Fortunate travelers with more time will divide the trip differently. The Parkway encourages everyone to investigate, to explore, and to enjoy. However much time they have, they will come away with an appreciation for this great historic highway.

The Natchez Trace encourages hikers to explore and enjoy all parts of the trail no matter the season.

★ COVERING THE NATCHEZ TRACE ON YOUR OWN POWER ★

It is still possible to walk much of the Natchez Trace. The modern trail does not follow the old one for most of the route. Only half of the original trail lay within the Natchez Trace Parkway when it was created in 1938. Eighty-five percent of that was destroyed by road building. This left about thirty-three miles of the original trace on protected National Park Service land.

The National Park Service began constructing segments of the trail in 1987. Three segments have been completed. A twenty-five-mile section in Tennessee is south of Franklin. A second twenty-five-mile section is under development north of Jackson, Mississippi. The third section, fifteen miles long, is near Port Gibson, Mississippi. These segments are limited to use for hiking and horseback riding. There are no fees for using the trail. Lodging, supplies, and medical attention are available in nearby communities.

The trail may never be a serious footpath. However, hikers often report enjoyment from roadwalking the paved Natchez Trace Parkway. More information can be gained by writing: Superintendent, c/o Natchez Trace Parkway, 2680 Natchez Trace Parkway, Tupelo, Mississippi 38804. The "Official Map and Guide" is free.

There are many scenic vistas for hikers, cyclists, and motorists to enjoy along the Natchez Trace Parkway. The waterfall at Falls Hallow is just one of these views.

The Natchez Trace Parkway is a great ride for bicyclists. It can be a day ride, a short "out and back," or a weeklong trek. The terrain is scenic, and wildlife abounds. Most of the route is flat, with rolling hills in the northern portion. There are many campsites and other kinds of lodging along the route. Rest areas, nature stops, and historical sites are frequent. Riders can get water at rest stops, and can go alone or as part of an organized group.

Riders are reminded that this is a highway. The speed limit for cars in most places is 50 miles per hour, and commercial traffic is not allowed. The road surface

In spring, the Natchez Trace displays a wealth of blossoms on dogwood and other trees.

is well maintained, but somewhat coarse and unfriendly to cyclists. The road does not have a bicycle lane, so bikers must keep to the right and ride in single file. It is advisable to wear a helmet, and not ride after nightfall.

In the early spring, the dogwood and redbud bloom along the trace. Summers on the trace are hot and humid, especially during August. The three most preferred months to visit are May, June, and October. Hikers and cyclists will find most folks along the Trace friendly and happy to share stories and information.

Over the centuries, the Natchez Trace has been a route for wild animal herds migrating to its great salt licks. Generations of American Indians used it as a trade route. Among the Europeans and Americans who traveled the Trace were explorers, soldiers, traders, boatmen, preachers, and robbers. Settlers found it a highway to the riches of the cotton empire. Today, visitors enjoy a sense of the past as they admire the beauty of the Natchez Trace Parkway.

★ TIMELINE ★

1542—Exploring Europeans make first contact with the Natchez.

1713—The French establish Fort Rosalie near the river at Natchez.

1729—Natchez American Indians attack French trading post, killing two hundred. French then capture four hundred Natchez.

1768—Watagua becomes the first white settlement in East Tennessee.

1783—The United States and England sign a treaty to end the Revolutionary War.

1784—Town of Nashville is established by North Carolina legislature.

1786—The Treaty of Hopewell establishes the borders of Chickasaw territory.

1793—Eli Whitney invents cotton gin.

1794—Act of 1794 establishes post roads and stage transportation. Private companies begin to build toll roads.

1795—The area around Natchez becomes American territory.

1796—Tennessee becomes the nation's sixteenth state.

1800—Natchez becomes an important Mississippi River port.

1801—The Chickasaw Indians sign a treaty with the United States to give it the right of way on the Natchez Trace. Samuel Mason begins his career as the Natchez Trace's most infamous thief and murderer.

1802—The government widens portions of the Natchez Trace.

1804 -1806—Meriwether Lewis explores the recently acquired Louisiana Purchase.

1808—Meriwether Lewis becomes governor of Louisiana.

1809—Abraham Lincoln is born.

1812—The United States declares war on Great Britain.

1820—More steamboats and a shorter route from Nashville to New Orleans spell the end of the Natchez Trace.

1830—Choctaws sign the Treaty of Dancing Rabbit Creek, surrendering 10.5 million acres in Mississippi to the government.

1843—Nashville becomes Tennessee's capital.

1935—Congress appropriates $1.2 million to begin construction of the Natchez Trace Parkway.

★ CHAPTER NOTES ★

Chapter 1. Traveling the Natchez Trace

1. William C. Davis, *A Way Through the Wilderness: The Natchez Trace and the Civilization of the Southern Frontier* (Baton Rouge: Louisiana State University Press, 1995), p. 16.

2. Ibid., p. 26.

3. Louis A. Warren, *Lincoln's Youth: Indiana Years, Seven to Twenty-One, 1816–1830* (Indianapolis: Indiana Historical Society, 1991), pp. 175–176.

4. Carl Sandburg, *Abraham Lincoln: The Prairie Years* (New York: Harcourt Brace & Company, 1926), pp. 83–89.

5. Robert Silverberg, ". . . and the mound-builders vanished from the earth," *American Heritage*, June 1967, p. 61.

6. Charlie Jones, "Sharing Choctaw History," Choctaw History—*Pushmataha*, 1987, <http://www.isd.net/mboucher/choctaw/push1.htm> (July 5, 1999).

Chapter 2. American Indians of the Natchez Trace

1. William C. Davis, *A Walk Through the Wilderness: The Natchez Trace and the Civilization of the Southern Frontier* (Baton Rouge: Louisiana State University Press, 1995), p. 3.

2. Alvin M. Josephy, *The American Heritage Book of Indians* (New York: Simon & Schuster, 1961), p. 158.

3. James A. Crutchfield, *The Natchez Trace* (Nashville, Tenn.: Rutledge Hill Press, 1985), pp. 46–47.

4. MuskogeeNet, "The Choctaw Nation," *The Five Tribes*, 1998, <http://fivetribes.com/hist_choctaw.html> (July 5, 1999).

5. Frederick Smoot, "A Walk Through Time," taken from *The Chickasaw and Their Cessions, TNGenWeb*, August 5, 1998, <http://www.tngenweb.org/tnfirst/chicksaw/walktime.htm>, (July 6, 1999).

6. Lori Finley, *Traveling the Natchez Trace* (Winston-Salem, N.C.: John P. Blair, 1995), p. 96.

7. Kappler, Charles J., LL. M., *Indian Affairs, Laws and Treaties, vol. II, Treaties* (Washington, D.C.: Government Printing Office, 1904; reprint, 1972), pp. 14–16.

Chapter 3. The United States 1760–1800

1. Henry Steele Commager, *Documents of American History* (New York: F. S. Crofts & Co., 1934), pp. 47–50.

2. Ibid., pp. 117–119.

3. Richard B. Morris, *Encyclopedia of American History* (New York: Harper Brothers, 1953), p. 410.

4. Commager, pp. 123–124.

5. Ibid., pp. 128–132.

6. *Historical Statistics of the United States* (Washington, D.C.: U.S. Bureau of the Census, 1960), pp. 7, 8, 14.

7. Morris, p. 419.

8. Thomas C. Cochran, *Concise Dictionary of American History* (New York: Charles Scribner's Sons, 1962), p. 540.

9. John Mack Farragher, *Daniel Boone: The Life and Legend of an American Pioneer* (New York: Henry Holt & Co., 1992), p. 70.

10. John S. Abbot, *Daniel Boone: Pioneer of Kentucky* (New York: Dodd Mead Co., 1872), p. 51.

Chapter 4. Southern Starting Point of the Trace

1. Joseph D. Shields, *Natchez: Its Early History* (Louisville, Ky.: John R. Morton & Company, 1930), p. 3.

2. Jonathan Daniels, *The Devil's Backbone* (Gretna, La.: Pelican Publishing Company, 1992), pp. 19–21.

3. Harnett T. Kane, *Natchez on the Mississippi* (New York: William Morrow & Company, 1947), p. 3.

4. Shields, p. 23.

5. Ibid., p. 50.

6. Kane, p. 127.

7. Robert Carson, *Mississippi* (Chicago: Children's Press, 1989), p. 42.

8. Robert M. Coates, *The Outlaw Years: The History of the Land Pirates of the Natchez Trace* (New York: The Macauley Company, 1930), p. 136.

9. William C. Davis, *A Way Through the Wilderness* (Baton Rouge: Louisiana State University Press, 1995), p. 72.

10. Daniels, p. 126.

Chapter 5. Nashville at the End of the Trace

1. Anita S. Goodstein, *Nashville: 1780–1860* (Gainesville: University of Florida Press, 1989), p. 2.

2. Lizzie P. Elliot, *Early History of Nashville* (Nashville, Tenn.: Ambrose Printing Company, 1911), p. 150.

3. Jesse C. Burt, *Nashville: Its Life and Times* (Nashville, Tenn.: Tennessee Brock Company, 1959), pp. 15–18.

4. Ibid., p. 23.

5. Goodstein, p. 20.

6. Jonathan Daniels, *The Devil's Backbone* (Gretna, La.: Pelican Publishing Company, 1990), pp. 61–65.

7. Tennessee State Library and Archives, Nashville, Tennessee.

Chapter 6. Hazards of the Natchez Trace

1. Robert M. Coates, *The Outlaw Years: The History of the Land Pirates of the Natchez Trace* (New York: The Macauley Company, 1930), pp. 129–132.

2. William C. Davis, *A Way Through the Wilderness* (Baton Rouge: Louisiana State University Press, 1995), p. 273.

3. Coates, pp. 151–165.

4. Davis, p. 276.

5. *Kentucky Gazette*, Lexington, Kentucky, September 14, 1801.

6. Jonathan Daniels, *The Devil's Backbone* (Gretna, La.: Pelican Publishing Company, 1992), p. 179.

Chapter 7. The Final Years of the Natchez Trace

1. William C. Davis, *A Way Through the Wilderness* (Baton Rouge: Louisiana State University Press, 1995), pp. 306–307.

2. Ibid., p. 311.

3. Jonathan Daniels, *The Devil's Backbone* (Gretna, La.: Pelican Publishing Company, 1992), pp. 216–218.

4. Robert V. Remini, *Andrew Jackson* (New York: Harper & Row, 1966), p. 72.

5. Daniels, pp. 225–226.

6. Leonard Huber, *Heyday of the Floating Palace, American Heritage*, volume 8, No. 6, October, 1957, p. 16.

7. Ibid., p. 17.

8. Davis, pp. 55–56.

9. Ibid., p. 56.

Chapter 8. Traveling the Natchez Trace Parkway

1. James A. Crutchfield, *The Natchez Trace: A Pictorial History* (Nashville, Tenn.: The Rutledge Hill Press, 1985), pp. 137–140.

★ FURTHER READING ★

Applegate, Stan. *Natchez Under-the-Hill*. Atlanta: Peachtree Publishers, 1999.

Crutchfield, James A. *The Natchez Trace: A Pictorial History*. Nashville, Tenn.: The Rutledge Hill Press, 1985.

Davis, William C. *A Way Through the Wilderness*. Baton Rouge: Louisiana State University Press, 1995.

Finley, Lori, *Traveling the Natchez Trace*. Winston-Salem, N.C.: John P. Blair, 1995.

George, Linda and Charles. *The Natchez Trace*. Danbury, Conn.: Children's Press, 2001.

Summerlin, Cathy and Vernon. *Traveling the Trace*. Nashville, Tenn.: Rutledge Hill Press, 1995.

★ INTERNET ADDRESSES ★

Bed & Breakfast Inns Online. *Natchez Trace Bed & Breakfast Reservation Service*. August 12, 1995. <http://www.usagetaways.com/natcheztrace/index.html> (January 17, 2001).

Crizelle, Kambre, Kelly, Lacey, Rachel, and Tyler. *The Story of the Historic Natchez Trace*. n.d. <http://tqjunior.thinkquest.org/6270> (January 17, 2001).

National Park Service. *Natchez Trace Parkway*. November 30, 2000. <http://www.nps.gov/natr/> (January 17, 2001).

Search US. *The Natchez Trace Parkway*. n.d. <http://www.searchus.com/parkway/> (January 17, 2001).

Thomas, Franklin W. *What is the Natchez Trace?* 1994. <http://members.aol.com/roadmusic/thomfilm/nthistor.htm> (January 17, 2001).

★ INDEX ★